LONDON
BY
TUBE

CHRISTOPHER WINN

LONDON BY TUBE

ILLUSTRATIONS BY MAI OSAWA

EBURY
PRESS

3 5 7 9 10 8 6 4

Published in 2016 by Ebury Press, an imprint of Ebury Publishing,
20 Vauxhall Bridge Road,
London, SW1V 2SA

Ebury Press is part of the Penguin Random House group of companies
whose addresses can be found at global.penguinrandomhouse.com

Penguin
Random House
UK

Text © Christopher Winn 2016
Illustrations © Mai Osawa 2016

Christopher Winn has asserted his right to be identified
as the author of this Work in accordance with the Copyright,
Designs and Patents Act 1988

Excerpt from *The Lonely Londoners* by Samuel Selvon (Penguin Books,
2006) on p. 215, reproduced by permission of Penguin Books LTD

www.eburypublishing.co.uk

A CIP catalogue record for this book is available from the British Library

ISBN: 9781785031502

Design by Peter Ward

Typeset in India by Thomson Digital Pvt Ltd, Noida, Delhi

Printed and bound in Great Britain by Clays Ltd, St Ives PLC

Penguin Random House is committed to a sustainable future for
our business, our readers and our planet. This book is made from
Forest Stewardship Council® certified paper.

MIX
Paper from
responsible sources
FSC® C018179
FSC
www.fsc.org

For Mai

ACKNOWLEDGEMENTS

All my thanks to the Home Team at Ebury – to Carey Smith for her insight and gentle guidance and for making this book happen, and to Lydia Good for all her help, enthusiasm, patience and ideas. Thanks also to Steve Dobell for his fine and sympathetic editing. Special thanks as well to Kevin for his support and friendship.

CONTENTS

PREFACE

By seeing London, I have seen as much of life as the world can shew

James Boswell

London is a city of surprises and variety, over 600 square miles (1,554 square km) packed full of character, spectacle and sensation. There are broad vistas and quiet corners, iconic sights and grand boulevards, historic buildings, quaint villages, verdant parks, smart squares, cobbled alleyways, museums, monuments, statues, markets, shops, theatres, cathedrals and ancient churches. Indeed, as Dr Johnson said, 'There is in London all that life can afford . . .'

Dr Johnson also tells us, 'If you wish to have a just notion of the magnitude of this city, you must not be satisfied with seeing its great streets and squares, but must survey the innumerable little lanes and courts.'

He is right. Really to know London you must look beyond the obvious, maybe venture a little further afield, be bold. London is so big and sprawling, and so full of places to see, that much about the city that is most interesting and appealing can be missed.

Of course, the best way to see London is to go by London Underground or, as it is affectionately known, the Tube. The Tube is itself one of the great sights of London. With 270 stations and over 250 miles (402 km) of track, the London Tube – first, best and biggest underground system in the world – can take you wherever you want to go in the world's most fascinating city.

London richly rewards the curious and the inquisitive and with *London by Tube* to hand, those who seek shall find . . . It unearths and explores a stupendous gallimaufry of interesting places – some well known, some less well known, some almost unknown – all of which lie within a short walk of a Tube station. There are surprising facts and untold tales, unexpected treasures, incredible monuments and undiscovered landmarks – indeed, for those who are prepared to sally forth and look around, London can offer up a truly amazing array of wonders and delights.

London by Tube

Each Tube line has its own chapter and there are stations from every line shown on the Tube map except for the Waterloo & City Line. Under the name of each station featured are the names of the Tube lines that serve that station, other than the chapter line. For example, Oxford Circus in the Victoria Line chapter reads:

OXFORD CIRCUS
Also served by Bakerloo and Central Lines

Each entry is headed with the following information:

NAME OF THE ATTRACTION
Opening times • Entry fee

The information about opening times and entry fees is just a guide. Opening times and entry fees are always changing; where relevant, the telephone numbers and websites of places of interest are listed in the Gazetteer so that readers may check for the current status.

All places of interest featured are within a short walk from the Tube station unless otherwise specified. Depending on the speed of the walker, a 'short walk' means no longer than 10 to 15 minutes. Places of interest that are worth a slightly longer walk are indicated.

The duration of the circular walks, such as that around Hampstead, depends on how long the reader stays at each place of interest on that walk, but each individual place of interest is still only a short walk from the station, unless otherwise specified, so that the reader may return to the station at any point on the walk.

Directions are given for each entry. Many readers will have a London A-Z with them (recommended) but the directions have been carefully detailed so that readers should be able to find their way to the place of interest without the need of a map. Where there are official signs to the place of interest this is indicated.

London by Tube takes you to 88 stations and some 150 different places of interest, viewpoints, walks, unique museums, historic pubs, ancient churches – if you want a day out and you want to do something different, then London is your town, the Tube is your means and *London by Tube* is your guide.

CHAPTER ONE

The Bakerloo Line

For there is good news yet to hear and fine things to be seen
Before we go to Paradise by way of Kensal Green

'The Rolling English Road', G.K. Chesterton

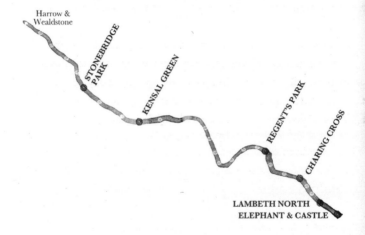

COLOUR: BROWN

YEAR OPENED: 1906

LENGTH: 14.4 MILES

FASCINATING FACT:

NAMED FROM **BAKER** STREET AND WATER**LOO**

North and west from Baker Street

WALK ONE

KENSAL GREEN
Also served by Overground

Britain's first garden cemetery

KENSAL GREEN CEMETERY
Open daily • Free

DIRECTIONS
Turn left outside the station, cross the Harrow Road and
turn right. After 200 yards (180 m) you will see to your
left a sign saying 'West London Crematorium, enter here.'

In the first half of the 19th century seven large private cemeteries
were created outside central London to ease the overcrowding
of the city's existing burial grounds, which were usually small
parish churchyards. The first of these huge suburban cemeteries, now known as the 'Magnificent Seven', was Kensal
Green, which opened in 1833 as Britain's first garden cemetery.
It was founded by barrister George Carden, who had been
inspired by a visit to the Père Lachaise in Paris. The General
Cemetery Company, which was set up by Carden to run Kensal
Green, still owns and manages the cemetery today.

Kensal Green covers some 72 acres (29 ha) with the largest
area set aside for Church of England burials and centred
around the Anglican chapel, a magnificent Greek Revival

building completed in 1838 which sits at the end of a wide avenue running from the main entrance. There is also an area for Dissenters with a Dissenters' chapel, the West London Crematorium, where singer Freddie Mercury and actress Ingrid Bergman were cremated, and two conservation areas. The Grand Union Canal runs along the southern border of the cemetery and this allowed coffins to be brought here by barge.

To wander through these peaceful green acres amongst the extraordinary array of strange and spectacular Gothic monuments – there are 140 listed buildings and memorials here – is an unforgettable experience, restful and yet somehow stimulating. There is also an element of the treasure hunt as you thrill to the discovery of some notable person's last resting place. Amongst the 650 members of the titled nobility and over 550 individuals featured in the *Dictionary of National Biography* buried at Kensal Green are Princess Sophia and Augustus Frederick, Duke of Sussex, children of George III, Prince George, Duke of Cambridge, grandson of George III and the last Duke of Cambridge before Prince William, Blondin, the acrobat who crossed the Niagara Falls on a tight-rope, engineers John Rennie the Younger (builder of the London Bridge now in Arizona), Isambard Kingdom Brunel and his father Marc Brunel (builders of the world's first underwater tunnel, *see* Rotherhithe), Winston Churchill's daughter Marigold, who died aged three and is buried beneath a monument by Eric Gill, authors Wilkie Collins, Anthony Trollope and William Makepeace Thackeray, playwrights Harold Pinter and Sir Terence Rattigan, Lord Byron's wife Anne, Oscar Wilde's mother Jane, the first W.H. Smith and Charles Babbage, inventor of the calculating machine.

As well as the normal burial plots there are three sets of catacombs, one of them underneath the Anglican chapel. For lowering coffins from the chapel to the catacombs the chapel has one of only two working coffin lifts left in England – the other is in the chapel of St Mary's Cemetery next door.

St Mary's Cemetery for Roman Catholics was established at the western end of Kensal Green in 1858. Amongst the notables buried here are Napoleon's nephew Louis Lucien Bonaparte, Sax Rohmer, creator of Dr Fu Manchu, nurse Mary Seacole, Cardinal Manning and Danny La Rue.

Guided tours of Kensal Green, including the catacombs, run on Sundays at 2pm. There is no need to book and the tour is free but a donation is suggested.

WALK TWO

STONEBRIDGE PARK
Also served by Overground

The first traditional Hindu temple built outside of India in modern times

BAPS SHRI SWAMINARAYAN MANDIR, LONDON
17 minutes • Open daily • Free

DIRECTIONS
Exit station, turn right and then left up slip road, following brown signs to Neasden Temple. At top, using pedestrian crossings, bear right and go over the bridge across

the North Circular. Cross slip road and turn left into Conduit Way. Neasden Temple is straight down at the end, about 15 minutes' walk.

Commonly known as Neasden Temple, this was the largest Hindu temple outside India when it was completed in 1995, and is the London headquarters of an organisation within the Swaminarayan branch of Hinduism called Bochasanwasi Akshar Purushottam Swaminarayan Sanstha (BAPS). London's first Hindu temple was opened in a converted church in Islington in 1970 but this building became too small after the city's Hindu population was swelled by Asians fleeing from Idi Amin in Uganda. The temple then moved in 1982 to a warehouse in Neasden, which was far from satisfactory, and BAPS leader Pramukh Swami Maharaj declared his wish that a marble temple worthy of London's Hindus should be built. Funded and built entirely by the Hindu community, Neasden Temple was completed in just over two years.

The Mandir, the temple at the heart of the complex, is built of Italian Carrara marble, Indian Ambaji marble and Bulgarian limestone, all hand sculpted in India. The pure, clean white of the building's interior highlights the intense colour of the monks' orange robes and of the golden shrines that are revealed from behind folding wooden doors, while a forest of pillars, carved with stories and symbols, soars upwards to an elaborate central dome.

Next to the Mandir is the Haveli, a cultural centre based around a vast hall used for prayer meetings and sports, made with gloriously carved English oak and Burmese teak. There is also a souvenir shop and a permanent exhibition called 'Understanding Hinduism', which explains the origins, history, traditions and philosophies of the world's oldest living religion.

Neasden Temple is a stunningly beautiful addition to the architecture of north-west London, rightly described by *Time Out* as one of the Seven Wonders of London.

South and east from Baker Street

WALK THREE

REGENT'S PARK

The Regent's Park covers 395 acres (160 ha) and was fashioned out of a royal hunting ground by John Nash between 1818 and

1828. It was opened to the public in 1835. Three sides of the park are lined with terraces, faced with white stucco, while the Regent's Canal runs along the park's northern boundary.

A WALK AROUND REGENT'S PARK
Open daily • Free

DIRECTIONS
Turn left on exiting the station, cross right over the Marylebone Road at the first set of traffic lights and walk straight ahead into Park Square West. Turn right at the end and left into the park. You are now on the Broad Walk. Running alongside are the formal Avenue Gardens, planted with seasonal flowers and decorated with fountains and statues. Continue along the Broad Walk to London Zoo OR turn left into Chester Road. Turn right into the Inner Circle and look for a small, discreetly signposted, entrance passage on the right, which leads to . . .

St John's Lodge Gardens, a secret garden ornamented with sculptures and ponds and a delightful place to escape the crowds and enjoy birdsong and nature. St John's Lodge was the first house to be built in Regent's Park, the second to be occupied, and is one of only two villas remaining from John Nash's original vision for the park. While the house is a private residence, the gardens have been open to the public since 1928.

☞ Return to Inner Circle, cross the road, turn left and right into . . .

Queen Mary Gardens. Named after the wife of George V and opened in 1932, these gardens contain the largest collection of roses in London, as well as a spectacular delphinium border, begonia garden, waterfall and lake. The best month to see the roses is June.

☞ In the north-west corner of Queen Mary Gardens is the ...

Regent's Park Open Air Theatre, Britain's oldest, professional, permanent outdoor theatre. It opened in 1932 with a production of Shakespeare's *Twelfth Night*. The auditorium, one of the biggest in London, seats 1,250 and many of Britain's greatest actors have appeared here including Vivien Leigh, Dulcie Gray, Dames Flora Robson and Judi Dench, Michael Gambon and Benedict Cumberbatch.

Leave Queen Mary's Gardens by the western exit past the restaurant and cross Inner Circle. On your right is The Holme, built in 1818 by Decimus Burton for his father and now one of the most expensive homes in the world. Ahead of you on the right is the Memorial Bandstand, moved here from Richmond Park in 1975. In 1982, during a concert by the band of the Royal Green Jackets, it was the target of an IRA terrorist attack, which killed seven soldiers and injured 24. Today there are regular lunchtime concerts here.

Walk towards the lake, bear left and cross over the lake via the footbridge on your right. (Baker Street station is a few minutes' walk from here.) Turn right and walk along the lakeside to the boating pavilion. There is boating here for adults and children between 10am and 6pm in the summer months.

Take the footbridge across the lake and bear left across the playing fields towards the zoo. On your left there are glimpses of Winfield House, built in 1935 on the site of a former Nash villa by Woolworth heiress Barbara Hutton. She sold it to the

US government for one dollar after the Second World War and it is now the US Ambassador's official residence.

☞ When you reach the Broad Walk turn left and walk to the road. Turn left for the entrance to . . .

LONDON ZOO
12 minutes • Open daily • Charge

London Zoo was founded in 1828, originally for scientific research, and is the world's oldest scientific zoo. It opened to the public in 1847. Managed by the Zoological Society of London (ZSL), which was founded by Sir Stamford Raffles in 1826, London Zoo can also boast the world's first reptile house, opened in 1849, the world's first public aquarium, opened in 1853, and the world's first insect house, opened in 1881. Amongst the zoo's famous inmates over the years have been Obaysch, the first hippopotamus seen in Europe (arrived in 1850), Jumbo the elephant, the first seen in England (1865), Winnie the bear, the inspiration for Winnie-the-Pooh (1914), and Goldie the Eagle, who caused a furore when he escaped into the park for 12 days in 1965. Today the zoo houses some 800 species of animal and a variety of animal attractions including Gorilla Kingdom, Tiger Territory, Penguin Beach, Rainforest Life with monkeys, sloths and armadillos, a butterfly house, an aviary, otters, hippos, lions, giraffes, elephants and more.

☞ Return to Regent's Park station along the Broad Walk (15 minutes) or follow signs to Camden Town on the Northern line (10 minutes).

WALK FOUR

CHARING CROSS
Also served by Northern Line

Two world-class art galleries and three extraordinary museums

THE NATIONAL GALLERY
Open daily • Free

DIRECTIONS
Take the Trafalgar Square exit and you will emerge into the south-east corner of the square. The National Gallery is on the north side of the square.

Known affectionately as the 'National Salt and Pepper Pot', in reference to the two small domes at each end, the National

Gallery building fills the entire north side of Trafalgar Square. The view from the gallery's elevated portico south across the square and down Whitehall towards Big Ben is spectacular. The building was designed by William Wilkins and the gallery opened to the public in 1838. Begun with just 38 pictures purchased from the estate of banker John Julius Angerstein in 1824, the gallery now houses one of the greatest collections of paintings in the world, with over 2,300 works. In 1991 the postmodernist Sainsbury Wing was added to the western end of the gallery to house the collection of Renaissance paintings. The new building was at the centre of a memorable controversy when the original architect's proposal for the wing was described by Prince Charles as a 'monstrous carbuncle on the face of a much-loved and elegant friend'.

Highlights of the National Gallery's collection include the *Wilton Diptych*, an altarpiece showing Richard II, painted for the King himself in 1395 and the oldest known contemporary portrait of an English monarch, J.M.W. Turner's *The Fighting Temeraire* (*see* Bermondsey, Jubilee line), Van Gogh's *Sunflowers*, Holbein's *The Ambassadors*, Velázquez's *Rokeby Venus*, van Dyck's *Equestrian Portrait of Charles I* and John Constable's *The Hay Wain*.

NATIONAL PORTRAIT GALLERY
Open daily • Free

DIRECTIONS

Take the Trafalgar Square exit from Charing Cross tube station. Climb the steps to the National Gallery and turn right then left into St Martin's Place. Entrance on the left.

The National Portrait Gallery moved here into its own purpose-built premises in 1896. It was the first portrait gallery in the world, formed originally in 1856 with 57 portraits, and it now owns the world's largest collection of portraits in all types of media – paintings, drawings, caricatures, sculptures, photographs and video. The primary aim of the gallery is as a historical record of prominent British people, with the fame of the subject more important than the quality of the picture, although there are many portraits by the great artists. The 9,000 or so portraits on display are arranged chronologically from the 15th century to the present day and there are frequent exhibitions by contemporary and individual artists in addition to the permanent galleries. Highlights include the Chandos portrait of William Shakespeare, which was the first work given to the gallery on its foundation in 1856, the only known authentic contemporary likeness of Jane Austen, a sketch by her sister Cassandra, Holbein's portraits of Henry VIII, self-portraits by William Hogarth, Sir Joshua Reynolds and Thomas Gainsborough, the anamorphic portrait of nine-year-old Edward VI attributed to William Scrots, which needs to be viewed from the right-hand side for the correct perspective, and the only surviving group portrait of the three Brontë sisters, an oil painting by their brother Branwell Brontë.

BRITISH OPTICAL ASSOCIATION MUSEUM
Advance booking only • Free

DIRECTIONS
Take exit to mainline station and go out across the
forecourt to Strand. Turn left and immediately left
between two sets of red telephone boxes into
Craven Street. Go down ramp and the museum
is the first Georgian house on the left.

Founded in 1901, this is the oldest museum of its kind open to
the public in the world. The museum covers the history and
development of optometry and visual aids for the human eye
and possesses some 20,000 related objects, including more than
3,000 pairs of glasses, from the 17th century to the designer
spectacles of today, spyglasses, eye-baths and other varieties of
corrective eyewear. Highlights include the only known pair of
Scarlett Temple spectacles in the world, made in 1730, spectacles belonging to Dr Johnson, C.P. Snow and Ronnie Corbett,
and some wonderful optical-themed cartoons by George
Cruikshank and James Gillray.

BENJAMIN FRANKLIN HOUSE
Open daily except Tuesdays • Charge

DIRECTIONS
Take exit to mainline station and go out across the forecourt
to Strand. Turn left and immediately left between two sets of
red telephone boxes into Craven Street. Go down ramp and
museum is a few doors down on the left.

Benjamin Franklin, author, diplomat, scientist, inventor and Founding Father of the United States of America, lived in this fine early Georgian (1730) terraced house in the heart of London for nearly 16 years from 1757 until 1775, when he was forced to return to America as the War of Independence loomed. From here, as a diplomat, he attempted to negotiate between the British government and the American colonies, making this house the *de facto* American embassy. This is the only one of his homes to survive anywhere in the world and since 2006 has been run as a museum dedicated to his memory.

Actually, it is not so much a museum as a theatrical experience. Visitors are shown through the house by a guide dressed as Polly Hewson, the daughter of Franklin's landlady. In each room a film is projected onto the walls with dialogue that tells how Franklin's life played out in that room – daily living and meals in the basement kitchen, social life and visitors on the ground floor, scientific work and political intrigues on the first floor. The visitor learns that Franklin was the only person to sign all four of the documents that forged America: the Declaration of Independence in 1776, the Treaty of Alliance with France in 1778, the Treaty of Paris establishing peace with Britain in 1783 and the American Constitution in 1787; also that while living in England he conducted experiments to prove that oil and water don't mix (in Mount Pond on Clapham Common), measured the effect of the Gulf Stream and invented the Franklin stove, bifocal spectacles, the harmonica, for which Mozart and Bach composed, and a new, more effective lightning rod – indeed he had a famous public squabble with George III about what sort of lightning rod to put on top of the steeple of St Bride's in Fleet Street. It seems a little unfair that we in London should be the ones to have this unique shrine to the 'First American', but we do and it makes for a fascinating experience. Booking in advance is advised.

HOUSEHOLD CAVALRY MUSEUM
Open daily • Charge

DIRECTIONS
Take Trafalgar Square exit and cross at the lights to the traffic island on your left. Now cross to your right to the round traffic island where the equestrian statue of Charles I stands. Cast in 1633, this was the first bronze statue in England and the first equestrian statue of a king. Today it marks the centre of London, from where and to where all distances are measured. Whitehall is ahead of you (with Big Ben at the end). Cross to the traffic island in the middle of Whitehall, then cross at the lights to your right and go down Whitehall. Horse Guards is on your right.

Located in Horse Guards, the official entrance to London's royal residences, the museum gives visitors the chance to see the working stables of the Household Cavalry (the Life Guards and the Blues and Royals) and watch the horses being groomed and prepared for duty. The museum celebrates the history of the regiment that has guarded successive kings and queens since the days of Charles II and plays such an integral part in the pageantry and traditions of Britain's monarchy. There are displays of royal standards, ceremonial uniforms, helmets and cutlasses, gallantry awards and musical instruments.

Highlights include items from the Battle of Waterloo, such as the bugle on which Lord Somerset's trumpet orderly, 16-year-old John Edwards, sounded the charge for the Household Brigade; a silver snuff box fashioned out of a hoof of Marengo, the horse ridden by Napoleon at Waterloo; and the cork leg fitted to the 1st Marquess of Anglesey to replace the one he lost at Waterloo – an irksome experience that provoked him to exclaim to the Duke of Wellington, 'By God, sir, I've lost my leg!' to which Wellington replied, 'By God, sir, so you have!' Other items include two silver kettledrums given to the regiment by William IV in 1831, silverware by Fabergé, and the bridle off Sefton, the horse who heroically returned to service after being horrendously injured in the Hyde Park IRA bombings and became the first horse to be placed in the British Horse Society's equestrian Hall of Fame.

WALK FIVE

LAMBETH NORTH

*Two gentle circular walks from Lambeth North taking in an art gallery,
a cathedral, a war museum, the world's first museum of garden history
and the life of the world's most famous nurse*

WALK I

Across the road in front of you as you exit the station is the
tall, white Lincoln Memorial Tower, opened in 1876 on the
centenary of the American Declaration of Independence by
Christopher Newman Hall, the pastor of Surrey Chapel, in
memory of Abraham Lincoln and his fight to abolish slavery.
Built into the spire are stripes of red stone intended to create
the impression of the 'Stars and Stripes' of the American flag.
This Gothic tower, which now stands alone, was built as an
integral part of a new home for the Surrey Chapel, originally
located in Blackfriars Road. Cross the road at the lights and
turn left, keeping the Lincoln Tower on your right. After
100 yards (90 m) on your right is Morley College, opened in
1889 with an endowment from MP Samuel Morley as a college
for working men and women. Today it offers courses in a wide
variety of artistic fields and is particularly noted for its music
and drama departments. A little further on and across the road
in front of you is the . . .

MORLEY ART GALLERY
Open daily • Free

Located in a former pub, this gallery puts on art exhibitions, events and talks throughout the year.

☞ Leave the gallery, turn right, and right again along St George's Road. After 100 yards (90 m) you will come to the entrance, on your left, to . . .

ST GEORGE'S CATHEDRAL
Open daily • Free

In 1852 this became the first Roman Catholic church in London to be raised to cathedral status since the Reformation and is today the seat of the Archbishop of Southwark. It was built in 1848 by Augustus Pugin, who became famous for working on the interiors of the Houses of Parliament and in particular for designing the Elizabeth Tower (the clock tower that houses Big Ben) and the clock faces of the Great Clock (known as Big Ben). Pugin was the first person to be married in St George's, in August 1848. The cathedral was badly bombed in the Second World War but was restored and reopened in 1958. Pope John Paul II visited in 1982 and the Dalai Lama in 1999. While the cathedral may be considered unremarkable from the outside, this is partly because it is hard to achieve a full view of it. The beautiful interior of tall, slender pillars, which seem to be marching like sea-sprayed trees towards the lovely stained-glass window at the west end, more than makes up for it. The acoustics are superb and ensure that the cathedral is a renowned venue for concerts and choir recitals.

☞ As you leave the cathedral you will see diagonally across the road the distinguishing dome of the . . .

IMPERIAL WAR MUSEUM
Open daily ● Free

Formerly part of the Bethlem Royal Hospital (Bedlam), this became the headquarters of the Imperial War Museum in 1936. The museum was established in 1917 to collect and display material related to the Great War and opened in the Crystal Palace in 1924. It then moved to the Imperial Institute in South Kensington before settling on a permanent site here in Lambeth.

The guns on the lawn at the entrance are 15-inch guns from the battleships *Ramilles* and *Resolution*, cast in 1915 and 1916, and the last survivors of their kind. Nearby is a section of the Berlin Wall, which divided East and West Berlin from 1961 to 1989. This section stood near the Brandenburg Gate and was acquired by the museum in 1991.

The exhibits inside, both permanent and temporary, now encompass weaponry, documents, artwork, films, photographs, sound recordings and books covering the two world wars and all military operations involving Britain and the Commonwealth countries since 1914.

Permanent exhibitions include the First World War Galleries, the Holocaust Exhibition, the Lord Ashcroft Gallery, which holds the world's largest collection of Victoria Crosses and George Crosses and tells the stories behind them, the Curiosities of War, which includes a section of the bar where the Dambusters crews used to drink, A Family in Wartime and Witnesses to War, where you can see a Harrier Jet, a Spitfire, a V2 rocket, a T-34 tank and a Reuters Land Rover damaged by a rocket attack in Gaza. Highlights include a Canadian Red Ensign carried at Vimy Ridge in 1917, Lawrence of Arabia's rifle, Winston Churchill's automatic pistol, Field Marshal Montgomery's staff car, and a midget submarine used to attack the German battleship *Tirpitz*.

The park that surrounds the museum is named after Geraldine Mary Harmsworth, mother of the newspaper baron Viscount Rothermere, who gave the land to the 'mothers of Southwark' in her memory in 1934.

Located a touch incongruously right next to the war museum, and well worth a visit, is the Tibetan Peace Garden, opened by the Dalai Lama in 1999.

☞ On leaving the museum turn left on Lambeth Road and cross Kennington Road. For the Garden Museum (Walk 2) carry straight on down Lambeth Road to the roundabout at the end. To return to Lambeth North turn right on Kennington Road and the station is at the end of the road.

WALK 2

Exit station and take the pedestrian crossing to your right across Baylis Road, then proceed straight ahead along Westminster Bridge Road towards the railway bridge. After about 50 yards (45 m) look across the road at the building with the wide stone arch, Westminster Bridge House. This was the entrance to the London Necropolis Railway station from where, between 1854 and 1941, the deceased of London were taken by train for burial in Brookwood Cemetery, near Woking in Surrey.

Cross the road to your left at the next pedestrian lights, turn left then right into narrow Carlisle Lane. Go under the railway and then right into Archbishop's Park, once part of the gardens of Lambeth Palace, the Archbishop of Canterbury's London home. The garden at Lambeth Palace dates from the 12th century and is the oldest continuously cultivated private garden in London – the remaining private section of the palace gardens, which can be glimpsed beyond a high wall at the far side of the park, is open to the public on the first Wednesday of the month between March and October, from 12pm to 3pm.

Walk through Archbishop's Park, keeping the play area to your right, and exit along a narrow passageway at the far end into Lambeth Road. Turn right and continue to the round-about at the end, enjoying glimpses of the Lambeth Palace outbuildings through iron gates in the wall on your right.

On your right, after passing through a small garden with a fountain in the middle, is the grand 15th-century red-brick Morton's Tower, gatehouse to Lambeth Palace.

On the right of Morton's Tower is the church of St Mary at Lambeth, now home to the . . .

GARDEN MUSEUM
Re-opens daily from 2017 • Charge

Founded in 1977, this is the world's first museum of garden history. The body of the church has been converted into an exhibition and event area with permanent displays of garden tools and historic gardening artefacts, and information on Britain's famous gardeners. The churchyard has been transformed into a knot garden around the splendid tomb of John Tradescant the Elder and his son John Tradescant the Younger, royal gardeners to the Stuarts and the first of the great British plant collectors who travelled the world looking for plants to bring home. Amongst those they introduced to Britain are the tulip tree, the plane tree and the pineapple – if you look at the columns on nearby Lambeth Bridge you will see they are crowned with pineapples in honour of the discovery. The Tradescants allowed the public into their home in Lambeth to see their unique plant collection, thereby creating the first public museum in England, and the collection eventually formed the basis of the Ashmolean Museum in Oxford, the establishment for which the word museum was invented. Its founder Elias Ashmole is buried here in St Mary's, as is Anne Boleyn's mother Elizabeth.

Also in the churchyard of St Mary's is the impressive tomb of Captain William Bligh, who was famously cast adrift in the Pacific Ocean by Fletcher Christian and the crew of HMS *Bounty* during a mutiny in 1789. Bligh and 18 loyal crew members survived 47 days in a small launch and navigated over 4,000 miles of empty ocean to reach Timor and rescue.

☞ On leaving the museum cross over at the lights to the Albert Embankment and turn right, keeping the river to your left. The short walk to Westminster Bridge provides spectacular views of the Houses of Parliament across the water. On reaching Westminster Bridge climb the steps to road level and turn right. Bear right into Lambeth Palace Road and on your right is the entrance to the . . .

FLORENCE NIGHTINGALE MUSEUM
Open daily • Charge

Located in the very hospital where she set up her training school for nurses, the Florence Nightingale Museum tells the story of the Lady of the Lamp, the founder of modern nursing, and traces the history of nursing. Highlights include the writing slate Florence used as a child, her pet owl Athena and the medicine chest she took with her to the Crimea.

☞ Exit museum, go straight ahead across Lambeth Palace Road, bear left and then right under the railway bridge into Westminster Bridge Road and return to Lambeth North.

WALK SIX

ELEPHANT & CASTLE
Also served by Northern Line

Unique museum of cinema in historic building

CINEMA MUSEUM
Open daily for pre-booked tours only • Charge

DIRECTIONS

Exit station and turn left, noting the grand
Metropolitan Tabernacle across the road. At the first
pedestrian lights turn right across the road and then left,
keeping a small park on your right. Bear right at the next
fork into Kennington Lane, take the first right into
Renfrew Road and the first right again into Dugard
Way. Walk on between the brick pillars and turn left.
The museum is a little way down on the right.

Now based in the administration block of the former Lambeth
Workhouse, where Charlie Chaplin lived for a while as a
child when his mother was destitute, the Cinema Museum
was established in 1986 in Brixton from the private accumula-
tions of cinema buffs Ronald Grant and Martin Humphries.
It houses an extraordinary collection of memorabilia related to
the cinema from the earliest days in the 1890s to the present
day, including posters, art deco cinema furniture, usherettes'
uniforms and hats, a popcorn machine, tip-up seats, old tickets,
film canisters, a 1912 Pathé projector, sections of carpet, a pair
of art deco entrance doors and even a container of the Floradol
perfume that used to be sprayed into the auditorium after a
show to mask the smells of nicotine and the unwashed. As well
as the permanent displays there are regular talks and presenta-
tions by film industry enthusiasts and film historians, classic
film screenings and live events.

CHAPTER TWO

The Central Line

When a man wants to write a book full of unassailable facts, he always goes to the British Museum

Anthony Trollope

COLOUR: RED

YEAR OPENED: 1900

WEST LONDON (WEST RUISLIP) TO NORTH-EAST LONDON (EPPING)

LENGTH: 46 MILES – THE LONGEST LINE ON THE TUBE NETWORK

FASCINATING FACT:

MARK TWAIN WAS A PASSENGER ON THE INAUGURAL RUN

West from Oxford Circus

WALK ONE

MARBLE ARCH
A Martyrs' Shrine

The arch from which this station takes its name sits rather forlornly in the middle of a swirling traffic system, an undignified fate for what was once a grand entrance to Buckingham Palace. The Marble Arch, made of white marble from Carrara, is modelled on the Arch of Constantine in Rome and was designed in 1827 by John Nash. It was moved here in 1851 to make way for the new east wing of Buckingham Palace that faces the Mall today.

The arch may look a little melancholy, but before it arrived much worse had happened here, for this was Tyburn, London's main place of execution. On the traffic island dividing Edgware Road where it meets the Marble Arch roundabout, there is a round stone plaque in the pavement which reads 'The site of Tyburn Tree' – the gallows. The first execution next to the stream known as the Ty Bourne took place in 1169, and then in 1571 the Tyburn Tree was erected on the spot, a much more efficient type of gallows on which several people could be hanged at one time. The first victim of the Tree was a Roman Catholic called John Story who was accused of being involved in a plot to replace Elizabeth I with Mary Queen of Scots. In fact, between 1535 and 1681, 105 Catholics were executed at Tyburn, including Oliver Plunkett, Roman Catholic Archbishop of

Armagh, and Jesuit priest Edmund Campion. A little way up Bayswater Road there is a plaque commemorating them on the wall of . . .

TYBURN CONVENT
Tours daily at 10.30am, 3.30pm and 5.30pm • Free

DIRECTIONS
Turn right out of the station, go across Edgware Road, noting the Tyburn Tree plaque on the traffic island, and on into Bayswater Road. The convent is 200 yards (180 m) along on the right.

Tyburn Convent is one of those places that make London such a uniquely fascinating city. Here, within spitting distance of London's heaving shopping mecca of Oxford Street, and one of London's busiest road junctions, is another world, a haven of peace and devotion where gentle nuns glide through quiet cloisters and contemplate in silence – how different from Speaker's Corner, just across the road, where they never shut up. In 1585 a priest, Father Gregory Gunne, visited the gallows at Tyburn and prophesied that one day there would be a religious house founded there to preserve the memory of the Reformation Martyrs executed at Tyburn. In 1903 his prophesy came true when an order of French Benedictine nuns, fleeing from religious restrictions in Paris, set up Tyburn Convent and established the Shrine of the Martyrs.

Today the convent is home to some 20 nuns of all ages from many different countries. They rarely leave the Convent, instead spending their days in silent contemplation and maintaining a vigil over the shrine. Each nun has her own room but life revolves around the chapel, where they sing Mass seven times daily and there is always a nun kneeling in prayer before the altar. Hanging in the chapel is a frame holding two pieces of wood: all that is left of the Tyburn Tree, which was finally taken down in 1783. Beneath the chapel is the Shrine of the Martyrs. There is a replica of the Tyburn Tree and around the walls are hung relics of the Martyrs, bits of straw and linen stained with their blood, pieces of skin or bone or hair, a fingernail, all taken from the bodies on the gallows, at great risk. One of the nuns is always available to take visitors on a tour of the shrine three times daily, at 10.30, 3.30 and 5.30 – ring the doorbell and wait by the staircase and she will appear as if by magic. The nun who guides you is allowed to talk and will answer questions about the shrine and life at the Convent. After time spent in this remarkable and refreshing place, where everyone smiles, the thought of returning to the noise and chaos outside is a little disheartening.

WALK TWO

EALING BROADWAY

Also served by District Line

An architectural treasure and the world's oldest film studios

Advertised as the 'Queen of the Suburbs', Ealing grew out of a small rural village grouped around the 12th-century parish church of St Mary's, while Haven Green, where Ealing Broadway station is, was a neighbouring hamlet. The town hall, the centre of the modern borough of Ealing, is situated between the two. Just to the south of the town hall is . . .

PITZHANGER MANOR

Open from spring 2018 ● Free

DIRECTIONS

Turn left outside the station and cross the road at the lights at the bottom. Turn right and walk along the Broadway, bearing left into High Street. After 100 yards (91 m) cross at the zebra crossing on your right, veer left across Ealing Green and the entrance to Pitzhanger Manor is ahead of you.

This is the best preserved of the many grand 18th-century country houses that graced this part of town, situated as it was on one of the main routes west out of London. Originally a large stone 16th-century house, Pitzhanger was remodelled in 1768 by George Dance the Younger for the Gurnell banking family, and then remodelled again in 1804 by Sir John Soane (*see* Holborn) as his weekend country cottage. Soane retained George Dance's wing out of respect, since Dance had been his first employer, but totally rebuilt the rest of the house as the magnificent Regency villa we see today.

After a major refurbishment of all the rooms, restoring them to how they would have been in Soane's time, the house will be opened to the public in spring 2018 as a museum, art gallery and exhibition space.

The grounds of Pitzhanger Manor have been made into a public park called Walpole Park, named after Sir Spencer Walpole, the last private owner of the estate. He was a descendant of Britain's first Prime Minister, Sir Robert Walpole, and grandson of Britain's only assassinated Prime Minister, Spencer Perceval, who had a house nearby at Ealing Common called Elm Grove.

The Manor and Walpole Park behind it are frequently used as a film location, partly because they are located right next door to . . .

EALING STUDIOS

Open occasionally for pre-booked tours • Charge

The world's oldest working film studios, predating the first Hollywood studio by ten years, Ealing Studios make Ealing the oldest centre of film-making in the world. The studio was founded in 1902 when pioneer film producer Will Barker bought The Lodge on Ealing Green and began making silent films in a shed in the back garden. Over the next few years he constructed three glass-covered production stages and by

1912 Ealing was the biggest studio in Europe. In 1913 the first British feature film, *Sixty Years a Queen*, about Queen Victoria, was produced at Ealing and in 1915 the first British epic, *Jane Shore*, which had a cast of more than 1,000 extras. In 1931 Ealing moved into the era of talkies when it was taken over by Associated Talking Pictures (ATP) and a number of proper sound stages were built, four of them, 2, 3A, 3B and 5, still in use today. Ealing Studios, as it became known in 1938, had its heyday in the late 1940s and early 1950s, when it was part of the Rank Organisation, producing a series of hugely popular, very English films known as the Ealing Comedies. These included films such as *Whisky Galore!*, *Passport to Pimlico* and *Kind Hearts and Coronets* in1949, *The Man in the White Suit* and *The Lavender Hill Mob* in 1951 and *The Ladykillers* in 1955.

In 1955 the studios were sold to the BBC and over the next 40 years some of their finest TV programmes were produced there, including *Colditz*, *Fortunes of War* and *The Singing Detective*. Since 1995 Ealing Studios has once more become an independent, fully integrated film and TV production facility, and on any day a stream of household names can be seen slipping in and out of the entrance. The studios are not open to the public, apart from the occasional organised tour, but the original house bought by Will Barker in 1902, which is still part of the studio and now called the White House, can be seen 100 yards (90 m) south of the entrance to Pitzhanger Manor, on the west side of Ealing Green.

East from Oxford Circus

WALK THREE

TOTTENHAM COURT ROAD
Also served by Northern Line

A circular walk from Tottenham Court Road taking in the world's most famous museum, two museums of comedy, one of the first Palladian churches, London's Tin Pan Alley, one of the world's most famous bookshops and some local colour

☞ Leave station by exit marked North Side of Oxford Street. Walk up Tottenham Court Road and take first right into Great Russell Street. Walk straight on for three minutes to the . . .

BRITISH MUSEUM
Open daily • Free

Founded in 1753, the British Museum was the first national public museum in the world. It began with a collection of some 71,000 objects, visited by 5,000 people a year, and now owns a collection of over eight million items, the largest collection in the world, and attracts more than six million visitors a year.

It all began with Sir Hans Sloane, physician to George II, founding governor of the Foundling Hospital, collector, inventor of Cadbury's drinking chocolate and the first medical practitioner to receive a hereditary title. In his will he bequeathed to the nation his collection of 71,000 objects accumulated during his travels around the world, in return for a payment of £20,000 to his heirs and the assurance that the collection would be put on show and not broken up. It was decided to create a 'British' museum to curate the objects, and on 7 June 1753 an Act of Parliament duly established the new British Museum.

Two libraries were then added to Sloane's collection, the Cottonian Library of documents assembled by Sir Robert Cotton, which dates back to Elizabethan times, and the Harley Library of manuscripts collected by the Earls of Oxford and Mortimer during the early 18th century. In 1757 George II donated the Old Royal Library of the kings and queens of England, later George IV donated the King's Library, and together these formed the bulk of what became the British Library.

The museum's first home was a 17th-century mansion called Montagu House, which stood on the site of the present buildings. It opened to the public on 15 January 1759, free for 'all studious and curious Persons', and has remained open ever since, except during the two world wars. As the museum expanded, Montagu House became too small and was replaced in 1823 by the vast edifice we see there now, which was designed by Sir Robert Smirke.

Even this huge building rapidly overflowed as the museum collected more and more items brought home from Britain's expanding empire, and in the 1880s the natural history collections were moved to a new purpose-built home in South Kensington to form the Natural History Museum. In the 1990s the British Library, which until then had been centred on the famous round Reading Room in the Great Court at the heart of the museum, was transferred to a new home next to St Pancras station. The old Reading Room was refurbished and is now accessible to all as an information and exhibition centre. The 2-acre (0.8-ha) Great Court was covered with a glass roof designed by Norman Foster and now forms the largest covered public square in Europe.

Famous items amongst the British Museum collections include the Parthenon (Elgin) Marbles, a 5th-century BC sculpted frieze from the Parthenon in Athens; the Rosetta Stone, inscribed with three different Ancient Egyptian scripts and key to helping scholars decipher hieroglyphs; the Mummy of Katebet, dating from 1250 BC and the best of the museum's impressive collection of mummies; the Lewis Chess Men, an exquisite set of 12th-century carved ivory chess figures discovered on the Hebridean island of Lewis; and the Golden Chariot, the glory of the Oxus Treasure, a hoard of gold and silver items from the First Persian Empire, 5th-century BC.

☞ Exit museum, turn left then first right into Bury Place. On your left is pretty Pied Bull Yard, once a stable yard now containing shops and a restaurant. Go to the end of Bury Place – the excellent London Review Bookshop is on your left – and turn right into Bloomsbury Way. After 100 yards (90 m) on your right is the ...

MUSEUM OF COMEDY
Restricted opening • Charge

Located in the crypt of St George's, Bloomsbury, this is the first museum in Britain dedicated to comedy and features familiar artefacts, props, posters, photographs, sheet music and memorabilia from the world of British comedy and comedians. It was opened in 2014 by Martin Witts, director of the Leicester Square Theatre, and revolves around his collection of some 6,000 items amassed during a career in comedy spanning three decades. Highlights include Steptoe and Son's stuffed bear, Charlie Chaplin's cane, the Two Ronnies' glasses, Bill Bailey's six-neck guitar, Benny Hill's mandolin and Tommy Cooper's hand-made magic props. There are regular exhibitions, photographic collections, an educational facility for aspiring comedy writers and performers, a licensed bar area called the Comedian's Arms and a 100-seat performance space and cinema for stand-up acts, pop-up shows and silent movies.

ST GEORGE'S, BLOOMSBURY
Open daily • Free

Consecrated in 1730, this was the last of the six churches built in London by Nicholas Hawksmoor. Often overlooked because it is hemmed in by buildings, the church's most notable feature is the steeple on the west side, which is stepped like a pyramid. The design was inspired by the original Mausoleum, the tomb of Mausolus at Halicarnassus in ancient Persia. At the top there is a statue of George I in Roman dress, and at the base of the pyramid are cavorting lions and unicorns symbolising the recent ending of the First Jacobite Rising. At the time, the church stood near a notorious slum known as the Rookery, and the distinctive steeple of St George's is easily identifiable in the top centre of William Hogarth's well-known engraving of debauchery, *Gin Lane*. The author Anthony Trollope was baptised in the church in 1824 and in 1913 the memorial service for Emily Davison, the suffragette who threw herself under the king's horse at the Epsom Derby, was held in St George's.

☞ Exit the church, turn right and right again into Museum Street, then left into Little Russell Street. At the end on your right is the . . .

CARTOON MUSEUM
Open daily • Free

London's only museum dedicated to cartoons opened here in 2006. Spread over three galleries is an ever-changing display of original, mainly British cartoons, caricatures, comics, illustrations and prints. There are rare historic examples by early satirists, such as William Hogarth, James Gillray and Thomas Rowlandson, works from Victorian artists, such as George Cruikshank and John Tenniel, and from early 20th century illustrators, such as H.M. Bateman and William Heath Robinson (*see* Pinner, Metropolitan line), as well as illustrations by more contemporary cartoonists, such as Gerald Scarfe, Ronald Searle and Giles. Upstairs is a display of original artwork from some of Britain's most beloved comics, including Dennis the Menace by David Law and Minnie the Minx by Leo Baxendale, both from the *Beano*, and Frank Hampson's Dan Dare from the *Eagle*. There are also some originals by Peanuts creator Charles Schulz. The museum runs regular workshops, events and exhibitions, and there is a library of some 5,000 books available for research, and a small museum shop.

☞ Exit museum, turn right then left and walk down to New Oxford Street. Turn right and 100 yards (90 m) down across the road on your left is the magnificent Victorian shop front of . . .

JAMES SMITH & SONS
Open Mon-Sat • Free

Europe's oldest and finest purveyor of umbrellas, canes and walking sticks was established in 1830 and moved here to New Oxford Street in 1857, since when the shop has remained virtually unchanged. This marvellously atmospheric emporium still trades from behind its original Victorian shop counter and retains its original Victorian fittings and standards of service. Umbrellas are made to order on the premises in a workshop in the basement, while walking sticks and canes are fashioned and cut to the correct length for each customer. No wonder London is considered the spiritual home of the umbrella and the walking stick.

☞ Exit the shop and turn left. Continue on New Oxford Street for 200 yards (180 m) and just before Centre Point turn left into Earnshaw Street. Ahead of you at the end is . . .

ST GILES-IN-THE-FIELDS
Open daily • Free

One of England's first Palladian churches, St Giles's church stands at one of the great crossroads of London, on the site of the chapel of St Giles's leper hospital founded by Matilda, wife of Henry I, in 1101. The hospital chapel also served the village of St Giles, which grew up around the hospital. In the 15th century the gallows from Smithfield were erected here and the churchyard became one of London's main places of execution, with the condemned offered a last bowl of ale, the 'St Giles' Bowl', as they passed the church gate on their way to execution.

The gallows were taken away to Tyburn, but many of those executed at Tyburn were sent to St Giles's for burial – amongst them one of the leaders of the 1715 Jacobite Rebellion, the Earl of Derwentwater, and the highwayman Claude Duval. After the Dissolution of the Monasteries in 1541 the chapel became the parish church of St Giles and in 1623 was replaced by a fine new building. This fell down when the walls were undermined by the diggings for thousands of burials made necessary by the Great Plague of 1665, which started in the St Giles district. A new church, designed by Henry Flitcroft, was opened in 1733 and this is the church that stands here today. St Giles's is sometimes referred to as the 'Poets', Church', reflecting the fact that poet George Chapman, translator of Homer, was buried here in 1634, with a memorial in the church by Inigo Jones, and the great 17th-century poet Andrew Marvell was buried in the churchyard in 1678, while John Milton's daughter Mary was baptised here in 1648, as was Lord Byron's daughter Allegra, together with two of Percy Bysshe Shelley's children at the same ceremony in 1815. The actor David Garrick married Eva Violetti in St Giles's in 1749. Luke Hansard, recorder of the House of Commons, was buried in St Giles's in 1828.

☞ Exit the church, go straight ahead then left and walk down . . .

DENMARK STREET

In the latter half of the 20th century this short Georgian street was the centre of the UK's popular music industry, known as London's 'Tin Pan Alley', after the area in New York where music publishers congregated in the 1940s and 50s – the sound of hundreds of new songs being bashed out on old pianos sounded like the banging of tin pans in an alleyway. The first music publisher to move to Denmark Street was Lawrence Wright in 1911. He went on to found *Melody Maker*. The *New Musical Express* (NME) was founded at No. 5 in 1952. Lionel Bart, writer and composer of the musical *Oliver!*, wrote here and became known as the 'King of Denmark Street'. In the 1960s the Rolling Stones worked on their songs at Regent Sound Studios, where Elton John wrote his first song, 'Your Song', in 1970. Donovan and Jimi Hendrix made their first recordings on the street and bought their instruments there. David Bowie recruited his first backing band at La Giaconda, a café in the street where musicians and publishers would congregate; Jimmy Page and the Kinks recorded in one of the basement studios; and the Sex Pistols rehearsed and recorded their first demos at No. 6. Today the music publishers and recording studios have gone, but Denmark Street is still lined with music shops despite being in the middle of a huge Crossrail redevelopment. If you listen carefully, you can sometimes hear the distant echo of a famous guitar riff wafting down the street.

☞ At the end of Denmark Street turn left into Charing Cross Road, and 100 yards (90 m) along on your right is . . .

FOYLES

One of London's most famous bookshops, and at one time the largest bookshop in the world, Foyles was founded in 1903 by brothers William and Gilbert Foyle. They first came to

Charing Cross Road in 1906, and in 1929 moved into Nos. 113-119 where they stayed until 2014. In 1930 William's daughter Christina initiated the celebrated Foyles Literary Luncheons to provide customers with an opportunity to meet their favourite authors. In the second half of the 20th century Foyles became famous for its uniquely antiquated shopping experience with shelves full of books categorised by publisher rather than author, old-fashioned hand operated tills and a payment system that forced customers to queue three times – it was so bizarre that Foyles became a tourist attraction in its own right. In 2014 Foyles moved just a short way along Charing Cross Road to No. 107, where 20,000 titles are displayed on four miles of shelves over four floors. The coffee shop at the top is a popular meeting place for artistic and literary folk.

☞ On leaving Foyles turn left and then left again past the old Foyles building into narrow Manette Street. Go through the arch at the end, turn right into Greek Street and walk past the ...

GAY HUSSAR

This restaurant has been serving Hungarian cuisine to left-wing politicians since 1953, when Aneurin Bevan began the trend. Legend tells us that Labour Foreign Secretary George Brown was thrown out for chatting up the female guests while Labour chairman Tom Driberg tried to seduce Mick Jagger there. In the 1980s the *Daily Mail* offered £5 to anyone who spotted Labour MP Roy Hattersley tucking in there and almost went bankrupt. Tony Blair was persuaded to run for the Labour leadership at table No. 10 by Lord Pendry in 1983, and New Labour spin doctor Alastair Campbell was rumoured to have installed a concealed video camera in the window opposite the front door to beam pictures of whoever went in direct to his office at No. 10. Former Labour leader Michael Foot celebrated his 90th birthday there in 2003.

☞ Next door, on the corner of Soho Square is . . .

THE HOUSE OF ST BARNABAS
Open occasionally for private tours

Here is one of the finest Georgian town houses in London, noted for its exquisite rococo interiors installed by one-time owner Richard Beckford, a son of one of England's richest families. Charles Dickens featured the house in *A Tale of Two Cities* as the home of Lucie and her father Dr Manette. It is now home to the House of St Barnabas, a not-for-profit members club dedicated to finding employment for the homeless, and is open on occasion for tours.

Now walk through Soho Square, originally laid out in 1681 as King Square in honour of Charles II, noting the half-timbered gardener's shed in the middle, the somewhat dilapidated statue of Charles II, which was removed to Grim's Dyke, W.S. Gilbert's home in Harrow, in 1880 and returned here in 1938, and the memorial bench to singer Kirsty MacColl who died in a boating accident in 2000.

☞ Go straight ahead and turn right into Oxford Street to return to Tottenham Court Road station.

WALK FOUR

HOLBORN

Also served by Piccadilly Line

A walk around central London's largest square, taking in two museums, an Inn of Court and a curious old shop

☞ Exit station and turn left into Kingsway, then first left into narrow Gate Street. Follow this round to the right into Lincoln's Inn Fields and turn left; 100 yards (90 m) along on your left is the . . .

SOANE MUSEUM
Open Tues-Sat • Free

On the north side of Lincoln's Inn Fields is one of London's most beloved and idiosyncratic attractions, Sir John Soane's Museum. To create the space in which to display his huge collection of antiquities and works of art, which he assembled with the help of his wife, a wealthy heiress, Sir John Soane, architect of the Bank of England and Dulwich Picture Gallery, demolished and rebuilt three connecting houses, Nos. 12, 13 and 14, over a period of 30 years from 1792 to 1823. In his will he requested that the resulting building should be opened as a museum with free access for 'amateurs and students', and maintained just as he had left it. Soane modified many of the rooms and devised ingenious ways to channel light and make use of the restricted space, innovations that he also used at his ground-breaking picture gallery in Dulwich (*see* Overground). There is a dome fixed with convex mirrors that reflects light to the deepest rooms of the house and a picture gallery where the paintings are hung on wooden panels that fold away, allowing for many more items to be accommodated in the small space. A random role call from this extraordinary collection, made all the more memorable by its domestic setting, might include the alabaster sarcophagus of pharoah Seti I dating from 1278 BC, architectural drawings by Sir Christopher Wren and Robert Adam, Canaletto's *Riva degli Schiavoni, looking West*, the original *Rake's Progress* by William Hogarth, sculptures by Chantrey and Flaxman, Sir Joshua Reynolds's *Love and Beauty*, a 13th-century Bible, Sir Christopher Wren's watch, and pistols belonging to Peter the Great and Napoleon.

☞ Exit Soane Museum, turn left, then right around the square. On your left is the gatehouse for . . .

LINCOLN'S INN

Open daily. Admission to chapel and precincts free – charge for tours

Lincoln's Inn is the oldest and, with its 11 acres (4.9 ha), the largest of the four Inns of Court. It has a recorded history that dates back to 1422, although it most likely began life even earlier, during the 14th century. It takes the name Lincoln from the Earl of Lincoln, adviser to Edward I, who owned a house nearby in Shoe Lane. The term 'Inn' refers to the accommodation kept for senior lawyers and their retinue of staff and guests staying in London when the courts were in session. The four Inns of Court are now associated with senior lawyers or barristers who are allowed to sit in court, while the remaining inns, such as nearby Staple Inn and Barnard's Inn, became Inns of Chancery, exclusive to solicitors and clerks. Lawyers in the early days were often clergymen and tended to build their inns around squares and courtyards like medieval cloisters. The garden squares of Lincoln's Inn make a tranquil haven and are lined with a medley of red-brick buildings from every age. The Old Gate House on Chancery Lane was built in 1517 and retains the old oak doors of 1564, while the Old Hall, one of London's finest Tudor buildings, dates from 1490. Sir Thomas More worked in the Old Hall for many years after he joined the Inn in 1496, and in 1619 John Donne, Dean of St Paul's and a member of Lincoln's Inn since 1592, laid the foundation stone of the chapel, which was designed by Inigo Jones and completed in 1623. It has an open undercroft where 'students can walk and talk and confer for their learning'. The Restoration of the Monarchy was first mooted in the undercroft, during a secret meeting of 80 Members of Parliament in 1659. In 1668 the antiquarian Elias Ashmole, founder of the Ashmolean Museum in Oxford, was married in the chapel to the daughter of fellow collector Sir William Dugdale. The Great Hall, largest in any of the Inns, was opened by Queen Victoria in 1845. Charles Dickens's *Bleak House* opens here: 'London. Michaelmas Term lately over, and the Lord Chancellor sitting in Lincoln's Inn Hall. Implacable November weather . . . Fog everywhere.'

The chapel is open every weekday, while the other buildings around Lincoln's Inn can be visited on a variety of pre-booked tours, except for the first and third Friday of every month at 2pm when you can just turn up.

☞ Exit Lincoln's Inn and go straight ahead along the south side of Lincoln's Inn Fields. Halfway along on your left is the ...

HUNTERIAN MUSEUM
Open Tues-Sat • Free

Lanarkshire-born John Hunter was one of the leading surgeons of the 18th century and one of the first to apply scientific observation to medicine. He was particularly expert at anatomy and built up a vast collection of skeletons and anatomical specimens, many of which are on display in the Hunterian Museum within the Royal College of Surgeons. There are also animal specimens and fossils, wax teaching models, surgical instruments and anatomical paintings and drawings. Highlights include the 7 ft 7 in (2.3 m) skeleton of the 'Irish Giant' Charles Byrne, Winston Churchill's dentures and the Evelyn Tables, a set of four anatomical displays of different parts of the human body that make up the oldest anatomical preparations ever found in Europe.

John Hunter's house in Leicester Square had two doors leading to two different streets, one for access to his living quarters and the other for access to his dissecting laboratory, and it is thought that this arrangement inspired the design of Dr Jekyll's home in Robert Louis Stevenson's *The Strange Case of Dr Jekyll and Mr Hyde*.

☞ Exit museum and turn left, then first left down Portsmouth Street for the ...

OLD CURIOSITY SHOP

The oldest shop in London, this delightfully crooked old house was built in 1567 and is reckoned to be the home of Little Nell, the heroine of Charles Dickens's novel *The Old Curiosity Shop*.

☞ Return to the square, turn left and right into Kingsway and return to Holborn station.

WALK FIVE

CHANCERY LANE

*A unique pub, the world's largest collection of silver,
London's oldest tailor and a medieval hall*

CITTIE OF YORKE
DIRECTIONS
On the north side of High Holborn, 100 yards
(90 m) west of the station.

There has been a pub here since 1430 and the present building,
from 1924, evokes an atmosphere of Olde England. The main
drinking area is unlike that of any other pub – a huge baronial
hall with a high-pitched wooden roof, first-floor galleries and
barrel-shaped cubicles along the wall where lawyers from the
nearby Inns can achieve a degree of privacy with their clients.
The bar is one of the longest in Britain, reflecting its previous
name Henneky's Long Bar. The poet Dylan Thomas drank
here – in 2014 a previously unknown poem of his was found
that begins 'This little song was written in Henneky's Long Bar
High Holborn by Dylan Thomas in 1951'.

LONDON SILVER VAULTS

Open Mon-Fri, 9am to 5.30pm, and Sat, 9am to 1pm • Free

DIRECTIONS

Exit station and turn left (west) along High Holborn.
Take second left into Chancery Lane and Silver Vaults
are two minutes' walk on the corner of Chancery Lane and
Southampton Buildings, to the left. Just walk in.

Here you can browse through the largest collection of antique silver in the world. Go down two flights of stairs and you emerge into a long, beige-painted underground corridor equipped with sturdy iron doors and lined with 30 specialist shops, each ablaze with glittering silver objects. Here is every kind of silver from household items, such as teapots, toast-racks, napkin rings, salt cellars and pepper pots, cutlery, and plate, to christening spoons, trinkets, jewellery, timepieces, goblets, bowls, picture frames and urns. There is Georgian silver and contemporary silver, most of it British but including items from all over the world. You can pick up a gift from as little as £10 or splash out on a set of Tudor spoons worth many thousands – or you can just gawp, for the atmosphere is friendly and informal and the shop owners are welcoming to those who just want to look.

The Vaults began life in 1876 as Britain's first safe deposit store, The Chancery Lane Safe Deposit, where Londoners could place their valuables for safe keeping while out of town or travelling abroad. In time, silver dealers began to rent the vaults to store their stock and then to invite customers down to have a look. Eventually the dealers decided to open shops where their stock was, and the Silver Vaults opened as we see them today in 1953 – most of the shops are still owned by the same families. The Vaults were originally watched over by guards armed with cudgels and cutlasses, and although the cutlasses are long gone they have never been burgled to this day. They even survived bombing in the Second World War that destroyed the building above. The Silver Vaults are a secret even from most Londoners and should not be missed.

A few minutes' walk further down Chancery Lane, at 93/94 is . . .

EDE & RAVENSCROFT

Located close to the Inns of Court, London's oldest tailors are specialists in legal dress. They were founded in 1689 and hold Royal Warrants for the Queen, the Duke of Edinburgh and the Prince of Wales.

BARNARD'S INN HALL

Restricted opening • Lectures free

DIRECTIONS

Exit station, and turn right (east) down High Holborn past timber-framed Staple Inn. About 100 yards (90 m) further down on the right, just before No. 24, there is an iron gate beneath a heavy pediment. Above the gate it says Barnard's Inn. Go down the passageway and you will come to the hall.

This beautiful late 14th-century hall, with Roman foundations, is located down a passageway off the south side of Holborn. It was the hall of Barnard's Inn, an Inn of Chancery associated with Gray's Inn, and is a rare survivor of the Great Fire. As a young man Charles Dickens lived across Holborn at Furnival's Inn, the site of which is now occupied by the former Prudential Building, and chose to make Barnard's Inn the first London home of Pip, the leading character in *Great Expectations*. Barnard's Inn Hall is the present home of Gresham College, London's oldest Institution of Higher Learning, which was established in 1579 by Sir Thomas Gresham, founder of the Royal Exchange, to provide public lectures on Divinity, Music, Astronomy, Geometry, Law, Physics and Rhetoric. The seven professors who lectured on these subjects held weekly meetings together and from those meetings evolved the Royal Society, formally instituted by Charles II in 1662 and the oldest scientific academy in existence. Gresham College still gives over 100 free lectures every year on an extraordinarily wide range of subjects, most of them in Barnard's Inn Hall. Anyone can attend and a programme of upcoming lectures is posted in the passageway to the hall.

WALK SIX

BETHNAL GREEN

MUSEUM OF CHILDHOOD
Open daily • Free

DIRECTIONS
Exit station, cross Roman Road towards the park
and walk north on Cambridge Heath Road for
3 minutes. The museum is on your right.

Here you can find the world's largest and most comprehensive collection of items relating to children and childhood, from the 17th century to the present day. The museum is a branch of the Victoria and Albert Museum and was opened here in 1872 by the Prince of Wales. On display are Barbie dolls and doll's houses, Action Men and Transformers, board games, slinkys, toy soldiers, teddy bears, puppets, the original Muffin the Mule, model cars including the famous Corgi Car James Bond Aston Martin DB5 with ejector seat, building blocks, children's clothing, prams, tricycles, famous paintings of children, and more. There are workshops and frequent special exhibitions, puppet show performances and play areas where different toys from the museum's collection can be tried out. The museum is not just for children but offers everyone a fascinating look at the changing cultures and preoccupations of childhood.

CHAPTER THREE

The Circle Line

*There was the Chapter-house, wrought as a church, Carved
and covered and quaintly entayled; With seemly selure y'set
aloft, As a parliament-house ypainted about*

Piers Ploughman

COLOUR: YELLOW

YEAR OPENED: OPENED AS CIRCLE LINE IN 1949. FORMED
OUT OF SECTIONS OF THE METROPOLITAN (1863) AND
DISTRICT LINES (1884)

LENGTH: 17 MILES

FASCINATING FACT:

IN 2009 THE CIRCLE LINE BECAME A SPIRAL LINE,
WHEN THE CLOSED LOOP WAS BROKEN AT EDGWARE
ROAD AND THE LINE WAS EXTENDED TO HAMMERSMITH
ALONG THE HAMMERSMITH AND CITY LINE. THE LINE
HAS NO TRACK OF ITS OWN OTHER THAN A SHORT
SECTION BETWEEN ALDGATE AND TOWER HILL

WALK ONE

MONUMENT

Also served by District Line

THE MONUMENT

Open daily • Charge

Here, close to the very spot where London began 2,000 years
ago, is one of London's oldest and best viewpoints. The tallest
isolated stone column in the world, the Monument was designed
by Sir Christopher Wren and was built between 1671 and 1677.
Erected in commemoration of the Great Fire of London, it is
202 feet (62 m) high and stands 202 feet from where the fire
began on 2 September 1666 in a baker's shop in Pudding Lane.
The reward for those who have the energy to climb the 311
steps to the viewing platform, which is 160 feet (49 m) above
the street, is a unique perspective of London, with old church
spires and modern glass towers competing upwards for the light.
The silvery River Thames snakes away towards the east and it
is easy to imagine it filled with sails and masts and noise. The

viewing platform used to be open, but after a spate of accidents and suicides it was enclosed by an iron cage in 1842.

WALK TWO

BLACKFRIARS
Also served by District Line

Blackfriars takes its name from the black robes worn by the friars of the Dominican priory established here in the late 13th century. The piers of the present Blackfriars Bridge, which was built in 1869, resemble pulpits, reflecting the area's monastic origins. The railway bridge next to it now carries the platforms of Blackfriars railway station and draws its energy entirely from solar panels; it is the larger of the only two solar bridges in the world, the other being in Australia.

Fleet Street takes its name from the River Fleet which flows into the Thames at Blackfriars Bridge. In 1500 Wynkyn de Worde, assistant to the printer William Caxton, set up a printing press off Shoe Lane to serve Blackfriars Priory and St Paul's Cathedral and so began the street's association with printing and newspapers – although they have now moved on, most of Britain's major national newspapers were printed on Fleet Street, and Fleet Street remains the generic term for the newspaper industry. Over time a number of hostelries sprung up on the street where the newspapermen could slake their thirst, and a few of these still survive.

A short walk from Blackfriars station takes in three historic pubs, the church that gave us the wedding cake and the house where the English dictionary was compiled

Turn right outside the station. Across Queen Victoria Street is the flat-iron shaped Blackfriar pub, built in 1905 on the site of the priory and identified by a Black Friar over the door. The art nouveau interior was created by the artist Henry Poole in glorious gold and red Arts and Crafts style with wood panelling, sculpted friars on the walls, a marble bar and intricate tiled friezes and mosaics. The pub was saved from demolition in the 1960s by Sir John Betjeman. Now walk up New Bridge Street, crossing over when you can, and at Ludgate Circus turn left into Fleet Street. On your left at No. 99 is The Punch Tavern, so named because the staff of *Punch* magazine, founded in the Strand in 1841, used to meet there. A little further along, at No. 95, is The Old Bell, built by Sir Christopher Wren for the masons who were rebuilding St Bride's Church after the Great Fire. Just past the Old Bell is a passageway leading to the burial place of Wynkyn de Worde.

ST BRIDE'S CHURCH
Open daily • Free

The passageway beautifully frames Sir Christopher Wren's tallest steeple, 226 feet (69 m) high and the inspiration for the traditional wedding cake. This is thanks to baker's apprentice William Rich who lived on Ludgate Hill in the 18th century and decided to model his own wedding cake on the steeple he admired every day from his bakery window. The design proved popular and soon became the accepted style for a wedding cake. Wren's church is the seventh on the site and has a small museum in the crypt, the Museum of Fleet Street, which preserves the remains of a Roman house and a Roman mosaic pavement found here during excavations, along with the foundations of the Saxon church and a display of medieval stained glass and ancient relics.

St Bride's has connections with the New World as well as the old. A bronze bust by the font commemorates Virginia Dare, the first English child to be born in the New World, who was delivered on Roanoke Island, in what is now North Carolina, in 1587. Virginia and her parents Ananias and Eleanor disappeared along with other members of Sir Walter Raleigh's mysterious Lost Colony. Also married in St Bride's were the parents of Edward Winslow – he became one of the leaders of the Pilgrim Fathers and was three times Governor of Plymouth, Massachusetts. Diarist Samuel

Pepys, whose birthplace is marked by a blue plaque in next-door Salisbury Court, was christened in St Bride's in 1633.

Return to Fleet Street, cross over and a little further along on your right, at No. 145, you will find the Olde Cheshire Cheese, which was rebuilt in 1667 after the Great Fire. It is famous for its gloomy interior caused by a lack of natural light, and with its brown glass windows and creaking dark wood and sawdust decor, is highly atmospheric. It was a favourite of Charles Dickens, naturally, and of P.G. Wodehouse. The entrance is down a small passageway.

☞ Continue along Fleet Street and follow the signs pointing right along narrow Johnson's Court to . . .

DR JOHNSON'S HOUSE
Open Mon-Sat • Charge

Dr Johnson's House at 17 Gough Square was built in 1700 by wool merchant Richard Gough. Johnson lived there as a tenant from 1748 to 1759 and whilst there single-handedly compiled his celebrated *Dictionary of the English Language*, one of the greatest scholarly achievements of all time. Published in 1755, it remained the pre-eminent English dictionary for nearly 200 years until the publication of the *Oxford English Dictionary*, which was first published in full in 1928. Johnson's Dictionary was used across the English-speaking world, in particular by the writers of the American Constitution. After Dr Johnson's time, 17 Gough Square served as a hotel, a printworks and a storehouse and fell into some disrepair before being purchased by the newspaper baron Cecil Harmsworth in 1911, restored and opened to the public. It is now run by a charitable trust and has been decorated as near as possible to how it was in Dr Johnson's day, with panelled rooms sparsely furnished with period pieces and pictures, a wooden staircase and a wonderfully tranquil scholarly atmosphere.

Everything in the house has a connection to Dr Johnson. Amongst the memorabilia are some exquisite portraits of Johnson in oil, one of them by William Frith showing Johnson meeting the actress Sarah Siddons, prints and drawings of Johnson's contemporaries and friends, manuscripts in Johnson's hand, including the manuscript of 'London: A Poem', written by Johnson in 1738, porcelain that belonged to Johnson's friend Mrs Thrale and his biographer James Boswell, Johnson's walking stick, letter case and portrait medallion. Since the museum is slightly off the tourist trail, and quite hard to find, the house rarely gets too full and there is usually ample time to sit quietly in the attic library pondering on Dr Johnson's great work – sometimes you can even hear his nib scratching . . .

Now return to Fleet Street, cross over and a little way along, just after Whitefriars Street is The Tipperary, established in 1605. It is the oldest Irish pub in London, having become an Irish pub in 1700, and was the very first pub outside Ireland to serve Guinness. Originally the Boar's Head, it changed its name after the First World War in honour of the song 'It's a long way to Tipperary', which was sung in the trenches by many of the pub's regulars.

☞ Now retrace your steps to Blackfriars.

WALK THREE

TEMPLE
Also served by District Line

A short walk from Temple station taking in two Inns of Court, the world's first tea shop, the monumental headquarters of British justice, a world class art collection, a quaint remnant of old London and a Roman bath (sort of)

DIRECTIONS

Exit station and turn left (east) along Victoria Embankment. Go straight ahead at the lights across Temple Place and then next left through the narrow gateway into cobbled Middle Temple Lane, which cuts through two Inns of Court, Middle Temple and Inner Temple, where lawyers, according to the poet Wordsworth, 'look out on waters, walks and gardens green'.

TEMPLE INNS OF COURT
Open daily • Free

The name Temple comes from the Knights Templar, a group of nobles who formed a brotherhood to protect pilgrims travelling to the Holy Land, and who owned the land here in the 12th century. All that remains of their presence here is Temple Church, built by the Knights in 1185 and one of

England's four surviving round churches – it was made round so as to resemble the round Church of the Holy Sepulchre in Jerusalem. Since it was featured in Dan Brown's *Da Vinci Code* the church has become a tourist attraction and now charges for entry. Middle Temple Hall is one of the finest halls in England, built in the 1570s during the reign of Elizabeth I, with a magnificent hammer-beam roof and carved screen of 1574. The first performance of William Shakespeare's *Twelfth Night* was given in the Hall in the presence of Elizabeth I. The Hall is open for pre-booked tours only, but is frequently used for filming and you may recognise it. While not many of the Temple buildings are open to the public it is always possible to enjoy a quiet wander through the gardens and courtyards of this peaceful oasis.

☞ Make your way northwards through Temple to Fleet Street and turn left.

At No. 1 Fleet Street is the sole branch of Child & Co, established in 1580 and the oldest bank in Britain still operating, although now as a subsidiary of the Royal Bank of Scotland. The memorial in the centre of the road marks where the City of London meets the City of Westminster, and when the monarch visits the City she or he stops here to receive the Sword of State from the Lord Mayor. Sir Christopher Wren's Temple Bar, the ornate gate that once stood here, now guards the entrance to Paternoster Square beside St Paul's Cathedral. At this point Fleet Street becomes Strand.

TWININGS MUSEUM
Open daily • Free

At No. 216, squeezed in between two taller buildings, is the distinguished white-painted doorway of Twinings, with the smallest shop front in London. Thomas Twining settled here as a young tea trader in 1706 when he bought Tom's Coffee House, which occupied the site, and to distinguish his coffee house from other coffee houses he began to sell tea as well as coffee. His tea proved popular and in 1717 Twining opened the Golden Lyon here as a shop selling tea and coffee for people to take home as well as to drink on the premises – it was the world's first tea shop. The noble doorway was built by Thomas's grandson Richard Twining in 1787 and incorporates the Golden Lion from his grandfather's original shop and two seated Chinamen as representative of tea's origins. Twinings (without an apostrophe), as written above the door here, is the oldest company logo in continuous use in the world, while Twinings itself is London's oldest ratepayer. Adjacent to the tea shop there is a small museum that tells the story of Twinings and of tea. Here there are cabinets filled with vintage tins, packaging, advertising and tea caddies, some of them lockable, dating from the days when tea was very expensive. There is also a counter where you can taste different teas.

☞ Now cross the road for the . . .

ROYAL COURTS OF JUSTICE
Open daily • Free – charge for pre-booked tours

Housed in this monumental building, designed by G.E. Street, opened by Queen Victoria in 1882 and star of many a TV news bulletin, are Britain's principal law courts, the High Court and the Court of Appeal. The interior is a wonder of Victorian Gothic, including over 1,000 rooms and a magnificent, cathedral-like Great Hall 238 feet (73 m) long. You can browse a small exhibition of legal robes and wigs, explore the nearly four miles of corridor or, for real drama, you can visit one of the court viewing galleries and watch a court case proceed – a list of the day's cases is pinned up in the Great Hall. There are also daily guided tours, but these are charged and must be booked in advance.

☞ On leaving the Courts cross back over Strand and turn right. It is 5 minutes' walk to Somerset House past the two island churches, St Clement Danes, mother church of the Royal Air Force, and St Mary-le-Strand, mother church of the Women's Royal Naval Service (WRENS).

THE COURTAULD GALLERY
Open daily • Charge

Located in the 18th-century splendour of Somerset House, once home to the Royal Academy of Art, the Courtauld Gallery houses one of the world's great art collections, that of the Courtauld Institute of Art. It contains some 530 paintings and 26,000 drawings and prints stretching from the early Renaissance to contemporary modern art and is especially rich in Impressionist and Post-impressionist artworks, having the UK's largest collection of Cézannes as well as masterpieces by Van Gogh, Gauguin and Monet.

The Courtauld Institute of Art was founded in 1932 by textile magnate Samuel Courtauld, who endowed the gallery with his Impressionist works to start off the collection. Co-founder Lord Lee of Fareham (who gave Chequers to the nation as the Prime Minister's country residence) later gave his collection of Old Masters, and over the years the Courtauld's collection has been added to by many benefactors, including works by Bloomsbury Group artists Vanessa Bell and Duncan Grant donated from the estate of art scholar Roger Fry. In more recent years the gallery has gained a large number of English watercolours. Amongst the highlights at Somerset House are

Manet's *Bar at the Folies-Bergère*, Renoir's *La Loge*, Van Gogh's *Self-Portrait with a Bandaged Ear*, Rubens' *Landscape by Moonlight*, Botticelli's *Holy Trinity* and *Two Dancers on the Stage* by Degas.

To return to Temple station go through the cobbled courtyard of Somerset House – you may recognise it as St Petersburg in the James Bond film *Goldeneye* – on through the central doors into the south wing and out on to the terrace where there are fine views of the Thames. Turn right on the terrace and at the end go left down the steps on to Victoria Embankment and turn left. At the far end of Somerset House go left into Temple Place. On your left is a scruffy narrow lane called Strand Lane where you can see, at the far end, one of London's hidden gems, the Old Watch House, basically 18th century and much in need of a lick of paint but still very attractive. It was used for keeping watch over the graveyard of St Clement Danes in Strand to prevent grave robbers. Beside it, glimpsed through a window, is what perhaps misleadingly is called the Roman Bath. It is most probably a 17th-century refurbishment of one and is fed by water from the nearby Holy Well of St Clement. Charles Dickens bathed here and in *David Copperfield* he has his hero plunge into a cold bath 'at the bottom of one of the streets out of the Strand'.

☞ Now go up the steps opposite into the gardens and return to Temple station at the far end.

WALK FOUR

EMBANKMENT
Also served by Bakerloo, District and Northern Lines

SAVOY CHAPEL
Open Mon-Thurs • Free

DIRECTIONS
After coming through the barriers turn left and exit station, then turn right into Victoria Embankment Gardens. Walk through the gardens keeping the river

on your right. At the far end exit the gardens and
turn left up Savoy Street. The chapel is 100 yards
up on your left.

Hidden away beneath the walls of the Savoy Hotel, the first
hotel in Britain to have electric lights and lifts, is the first
church in Britain to have electric lights, the Savoy Chapel,
which was electrified in 1890. Built in 1512, the chapel is all
that remains of a hospital for the poor founded by Henry VII
on the site of John of Gaunt's Savoy Palace, which was swept
away by the mob during the Peasants' Revolt in 1381. As part
of the Savoy Estate it is the only working church owned by the
Duchy of Lancaster and is actually a private chapel that falls
under the jurisdiction of the monarch, although still within the
Church of England. Its proper title is the Queen's Chapel of
the Savoy. The National Anthem is sung at every service, but
using the words 'Long live our noble Duke', rather than Queen
or King, since the monarch here is addressed as the Duke of
Lancaster. In Victorian days the chapel was a hugely fashionable place to be married, as well as somewhere divorced people
could marry since it did not require banns to be announced. In
Evelyn Waugh's *Brideshead Revisited* the chapel is described as
'the place where divorced couples got married in those days –
a poky little place'. It is no longer poky but simple and quite
beautiful after some ten years of restoration. The ceiling, newly
repainted in bright blue and gold Tudor pattern, is sumptuous.
By order of George VI it is the Chapel of the Royal Victorian
Order and, unusually, is aligned north/south rather than the
traditional east/west.

WALK FIVE

WESTMINSTER
Also served by District and Jubilee Lines

*The Mother of Parliaments, the oldest garden in England,
two ancient treasuries and a wartime bunker*

This is the station for the Houses of Parliament, which can be explored on a pre-booked guided tour on Saturdays or weekdays in summer, and Westminster Abbey, where every British monarch has been crowned since William the Conqueror in 1066. Thanks to televised royal weddings and funerals the Abbey is probably the world's most widely recognised church after St Peter's in Rome, and yet it still manages to keep a few secrets.

WESTMINSTER ABBEY CHAPTER HOUSE AND PYX CHAMBER
English Heritage • Open Mon-Sat • Free

DIRECTIONS
Take Bridge Street exit to emerge opposite Big Ben and turn right. Cross left at the lights – here you are close to where the world's first traffic light was set up in 1868, while Parliament Square was designated as Britain's first roundabout in 1926. Continue past the policemen guarding the entrance to the Houses of Parliament and at the next lights cross the road to your right. Go left and right past St Margaret's Church into the Abbey close. Go to the end of the Abbey, turn

left into the Sanctuary and go through the archway
diagonally in front of you into Dean's Yard. Turn left
and the entrance to the Cloisters and Chapter House
is ahead of you.

The octagonal Chapter House of Westminster Abbey is one
of the most important buildings in Britain's history, for it is the
birthplace of the Mother of Parliaments. It was in the Chapter
House, on 20 January 1265, that Simon de Montfort held the first
representative Parliament, which led in time to the formation of
the Commons. The Commons itself met in the Chapter House

from 1352 until 1397. The Chapter House was built in 1250 as part of Henry III's great remodelling of Edward the Confessor's Norman church and was designed for the use of the Benedictine monks of the Abbey for their daily meetings and for the King's Great Council. For this reason it remains under the jurisdiction of Parliament rather than the Abbey and is now in the care of English Heritage. The beautifully vaulted ceiling splays out from a slender central column. One of the doors comes from the original Saxon church and dates from 1050, making it possibly the oldest door in England. Much of the floor is composed of 13th-century glazed tiles and there are some superb 14th-century paintings in the wall arcades depicting the Last Judgement, the Apocalypse and the Revelation. It takes your breath away.

Next door is the Pyx Chamber, which formed the undercroft of the monks' dormitory and dates from the 11th century. This served as a treasury for both the Abbey and the Crown and retains a 13th-century stone altar and medieval tiled floor that survived the Reformation.

WESTMINSTER ABBEY GARDEN

The Abbey has three gardens: the Garth, a green lawn bounded by the Cloisters, which was designed to rest the monks' eyes and minds as they walked around it; the Little Cloister Garden, with scented flowers and a tinkling fountain at the centre, set aside for rest and recuperation; and College Garden, the oldest cultivated garden in England, where medicinal herbs and plants were grown to help the monks' physical health. Admission to the Cloisters is free and College Garden is usually open for a few hours in the middle of the week.

THE JEWEL TOWER
English Heritage • Open daily • Charge

DIRECTIONS
As for the Abbey Cloisters, but do not turn right
past St Margaret's into the Abbey close. Instead go
straight ahead and the Jewel Tower is immediately
on your right.

The Palace of Westminster has its secret places too, and the
Jewel Tower is the one that is open to the public. It was built
in 1365 to house Edward III's private treasury and is one of
only four surviving parts of the old Palace of Westminster, the
others being the Chapel of St Mary's Undercroft, St Stephen's
Cloisters and Chapter House and Richard II's Westminster
Hall. The Tower had a moat and was built on land appropri-
ated from the Abbey, much to the monks' displeasure. Perhaps
it was divine retribution that William Usshebourne, the Keeper
of the Privy Palace, who had recommended Edward to put the
Tower there and had stocked the moat with fresh fish, should
expire while eating a pike taken from its waters. In 1512 there
was a fire in the Palace of Westminster and Henry VIII decided
to move his possessions up the road to Whitehall Palace – thus
ending the Palace of Westminster's role as a royal residence.
From 1621 until the new Houses of Parliament were ready in
the 1850s, the Jewel Tower was used to house Parliamentary
records, now stored in the Victoria Tower.

Today the Tower is interesting for its original 14th-century
ribbed vault, a display of robes of the Speaker of the House
of Commons, an exhibition of historic weights and measures
and an interactive touch-screen display about the history of the

Houses of Parliament. Being somewhat off the obvious tourist trail, it is rarely overcrowded.

CHURCHILL WAR ROOMS
Open daily • Charge

DIRECTIONS
Take Bridge Street exit to emerge opposite Big Ben
and turn right. Go straight ahead across Parliament
Street at the lights, turn right and left into King Charles
Street. The Churchill War Rooms are on the left
down the steps at the end.

Buried deep under the Treasury Building in Whitehall, the Churchill War Rooms were constructed as underground emergency accommodation for Winston Churchill's War Cabinet and the Chiefs of Staff of Britain's armed forces during the Second World War. They became operational on 27 August 1939, just one week before Britain declared war on Germany, and stayed in use 24 hours a day as the nerve centre of Britain's war effort until the Japanese surrender in August 1945, when the lights were finally turned off for the first time in over six years. It had originally been envisaged that the Cabinet would move out of London, but Churchill decided that this would be bad for morale and so the Cabinet stayed put, meeting in these war rooms 115 times.

Today the site is managed as part of the Imperial War Museum and visitors can see the 19 rooms that formed the nucleus of the headquarters, including the Cabinet Room, the Transatlantic Telephone Room from where Churchill could keep in touch with President Roosevelt, the Map Room, manned day and night and where vital information was collated and interpreted, and the Prime Minister's Room – Churchill's bedroom and office from where he made many of his famous wartime broadcasts. The War Rooms opened to the public in 1984, and in 2005 the Queen opened the adjacent Churchill Museum, an area given over to material exploring the life and work of the man voted the Greatest Briton of all time, Winston Churchill.

WALK SIX

ST JAMES'S PARK

Also served by District Line

GUARDS MUSEUM

Open daily • Charge

DIRECTIONS

After clearing the barriers turn left for the exit. Cross the road and go straight ahead into Queen Anne's Gate, a delightful street of well-preserved Queen Anne houses, on through the gate at the end (also called Queen Anne's Gate) and left onto Birdcage Walk, so named as it was the site of James I's aviary. The museum is on your left after 200 yards (180 m), in the grounds of Wellington Barracks. Next door is the Guards Chapel, rebuilt in 1960 after a flying bomb landed on it in 1944, causing 121 deaths.

Opened in 1988, the Guards Museum tells the story of the five regiments of Foot Guards: the Grenadier Guards (*see*

Hyde Park Corner, Piccadilly Line), Coldstream Guards, Scots Guards, Irish Guards and Welsh Guards. Along with the two regiments of the Household Cavalry (*see* Charing Cross, Bakerloo line) the Foot Guards have been responsible for guarding the Sovereign and the royal palaces since the 17th century and it is these soldiers who are seen standing in their sentry boxes outside Buckingham Palace and St James's Palace, or parading in their red jackets and tall bearskin hats during ceremonies such as the Trooping the Colour. The museum has a fine collection of historic Guards uniforms alongside paintings, weaponry, sculptures and artefacts illustrating the history and way of life of the Guards and showing that they are not just ceremonial but genuine fighting soldiers as well.

WALK SEVEN

SOUTH KENSINGTON

Also served by District and Piccadilly Lines

Here is Britain's largest concentration of museums, built upon the legacy of the Great Exhibition in Hyde Park in 1851. *The Times* coined the name Albertopolis for the area around Exhibition Road in recognition of Prince Albert's leading role in promoting and organising the Exhibition and establishing the museums. The Victoria & Albert, the world's largest museum of art and design, was founded in 1852 and its first director was Henry Cole, the inventor of the Christmas card. It has a permanent collection of some 4,500 objects, the largest collection of Italian Renaissance items outside Italy and the largest collection of Islamic artworks in the western world. The Science Museum, founded in 1857, is where you can see Stephenson's Rocket and Puffing Billy, the world's oldest surviving steam locomotive, the first jet engine, and the first working model of Charles Babbage's calculating machine, ancestor of the modern computer. The Natural History Museum was opened in 1881 to house the natural history collection of the British Museum. To visit one of the less well-known museums, walk north up Exhibition Road, turn left into Prince Consort Road and on your left is the Royal College of Music where you will find their . . .

MUSEUM OF MUSIC
Open Tues-Fri • Free

The Royal College of Music was established in 1882 to teach all aspects of Western music from undergraduate to doctorate level. Over the years it has built up one of Britain's most comprehensive collections of musical instruments, consisting of over 1,000 instruments dating from the 15th century to the present day, as well as manuscripts, paintings and photographs of well-known composers and musicians. The collection was started with the help of a donation in 1884 of nearly 100 Indian instruments from Calcutta music scholar and teacher Rajah Sourindro Mohun Tagore, who was keen to integrate Western and Indian music, and another donation a few years later of some 200 instruments from the collector Sir George Donaldson. Here you can see the world's earliest surviving stringed keyboard instrument, the anonymous clavicytherium, which dates from around 1480, a harpsichord by Alessandro Trasuntino from 1531, a 1591 guitar by Belchior Dias, a Division Viol (a type of bass stringed instrument) by Barak Norman from 1692 and a Broadwood Grand Piano of 1799, as well as trombones played by Gustav Holst and Sir Edward Elgar. Many of the instruments are kept in playing condition and the college holds regular workshops and concerts during which the instruments can be heard.

WALK EIGHT

HIGH STREET KENSINGTON
Also served by District Line

A new design, a private palace of art and a glimpse of domestic Victoriana

DESIGN MUSEUM
Open daily • Free

DIRECTIONS
Exit station and turn left down High Street. After 400 yards (366 m), the museum is directly across the road from the ODEON.

The Design Museum was established in 1989 to showcase contemporary and innovative design in all fields – fashion, industry, automotive, architecture and graphic design – and was the first museum in the world to have an important section on the design of mass-produced products. The museum moved to Kensington in 2016 from its previous home, a converted warehouse on the south bank of the Thames near Tower Bridge, when the old site became too small. The new building formerly housed the Commonwealth Institute and when it was built in 1962 it was considered an architectural marvel, clad with glass and a Zambian copper roof. It was remodelled, while remaining true to the original building, using innovative design techniques to become a fitting home for the Design Museum. On view are concept items and design favourites: cars, radios, clocks and watches, clothing, furniture, toys and a huge range of everyday items along with notes on the ideas behind their design and development. The venue is spectacular and certainly helps to enhance the displays.

☞ Exit museum and turn right (west) onto High Street. After 200 yards (183 m) turn right into Melbury Road and then left into Holland Park Road. 100 yards (91 m) down, on the right is . . .

LEIGHTON HOUSE MUSEUM
Open daily except Tuesdays • Charge

Frederic, Lord Leighton was the grandson of the senior physician to the Russian royal family and an independently wealthy man, but he was determined to become an eminent artist purely on merit, an ambition he achieved in spectacular fashion when Queen Victoria bought his first major painting in 1855; he became president of the Royal Academy in 1878, and is the only British artist ever to be elevated to the peerage. He is buried in St Paul's Cathedral.

Leighton House appears to be a simple red-brick house, but inside is a 'private palace of art', centred around the huge first-floor north-facing studio of Lord Leighton and a spectacular Arab Hall decorated with mosaics and Islamic tiles brought back by the artist from the Middle East and set beneath a golden dome. Leighton House was built by George Aitchison to Lord Leighton's personal specifications over a period of 30 years and is the only such studio home open to the public in Britain. It made its debut as a public museum in 1929, and on display in the house at any one time are a selection from the museum's collection of 76 oil paintings and 700 sketches and drawings by Lord Leighton, as well as sculptures, pottery and works by members of the Pre-Raphaelites who were friends of Lord Leighton, such as John Everett Millais and Edward Burne-Jones. There are also works by G.F. Watts, James McNeill Whistler and Byam Shaw.

Leighton House sits at the centre of the Holland Park Circle, a group of studio homes built in the vicinity by leading Victorian artists, many of which have survived. The only one deliberately destroyed was that belonging to G.F. Watts, which was pulled down in 1964 to make way for a block of flats. Backing onto the garden of Leighton House is 8 Melbury Road, designed by Norman Shaw in Queen Anne style for artist Marcus Stone. There are two more interesting examples in Melbury Road. The Tower House at No. 29 was built for himself by artist and architect William Burges in 1875, and has since been lived in by Poet Laureate Sir John Betjeman, actor Richard Harris and Led Zeppelin guitarist Jimmy Page. Next door at No. 31, again by Norman Shaw, is the former studio home of artist Sir Samuel Luke Fildes. It has 47 rooms, including the studio where Edward VII sat for a portrait – thought by a subsequent owner, film director Michael Winner, to be the finest room in London. He used it as his bedroom.

☞ Exit museum, retrace steps to High Street and turn left (east) back towards tube station. Just past the Design Museum turn left into Phillimore Gardens and second right into Stafford Terrace – on your right at No. 18 is . . .

LINLEY SAMBOURNE'S HOUSE

Open Wed, Sat and Sun, guided tours only • Other days pre-booked tour only • Charge

No. 18 Stafford Terrace was the home of *Punch* cartoonist Linley Sambourne and his family from 1875 until his death in 1910. He decorated the house in Aesthetic style, filling the rooms with Oriental and Middle Eastern objects and influences. Along with examples of blue-and-white Chinese porcelain and Japanese artworks there are stained-glass windows and rooms lined with William Morris wallpaper. Sambourne's children preserved the house almost exactly as their father left it, and today it provides a unique example of a period late-Victorian terraced house. Sambourne's grand-daughter Anne, Countess of Rosse, was inspired by the house to found the Victorian Society, dedicated to the preservation of Victorian and Edwardian architecture and art. The Society held their first meeting at 18 Stafford Terrace in 1958, when the founder members present included Sir John Betjeman and Nikolaus Pevsner.

CHAPTER FOUR

The District Line

I think that the poorest he that is in England hath a life to live, as the greatest he

Colonel Thomas Rainsborough: The Putney Debates

COLOUR: GREEN

YEAR OPENED: 1868, THE SECOND LINE TO OPEN

LENGTH: 40 MILES

FASCINATING FACT:

THE FIRST ESCALATOR ON THE UNDERGROUND
NETWORK WAS INTRODUCED AT EARL'S COURT
STATION ON THE DISTRICT LINE IN 1911 AND A
ONE-LEGGED MAN CALLED BUMPER HARRIS WAS
HIRED TO TRAVEL UP AND DOWN ON THE
NEWFANGLED MOVING STAIRCASE ALL DAY
TO PROVE THAT IT WAS SAFE

West – Wimbledon Branch

WALK ONE

PUTNEY BRIDGE

A forgotten palace and a forgotten moment in Britain's history

FULHAM PALACE
Open daily • Free

DIRECTIONS

Exit station and turn right then left down Gonville Street to Putney Bridge. Cross over towards All Saints Church at the lights, go left and then right through the stone gates into Bishops Park. Walk along the river with Fulham Palace on your right and follow signs to the entrance.

Set in 27 acres (11 ha) of glorious garden beside the river, Fulham Palace is a real hidden delight. The Bishops of London have held land here since Saxon days and used Fulham as a summer residence from as long ago as the 11th or 12th century. The last Bishop to live in the palace left in 1973 and the present Bishop of London now resides in the Old Deanery near St Paul's Cathedral.

Fulham Palace today is a pleasing mix of Tudor and Georgian architecture with a Victorian chapel. The Tudor buildings are grouped around the attractive west courtyard and include a splendid Great Hall of 1495 entered via an early 16th-century porch with clock tower. The Georgian east wing was built around the original east courtyard in the mid-18th century and remodelled in 1915. The chapel, the fourth one at Fulham, was built in 1867 and restored after bomb damage in the Second World War.

The Georgian rooms house a museum charting the history of the Fulham Palace site and there are frequent guided tours around the palace and gardens for a small fee. There is also a museum shop in the stately Porteus Library.

The Fulham Palace grounds, a portion of which have been hived off to make Bishops Park, were once enclosed by the longest moat in Britain, thought to have been dug as a defensive measure by the Romans. During the 16th and 17th centuries the gardens became famous as one of the world's first and most significant botanical gardens, planted with new species of plants and trees sent back from overseas by representatives of the Church of England for whom the Bishop of London was responsible. Europe's first tamarisk tree was planted here in 1560, and later the first magnolia and the first maple, introduced by renowned botanist Bishop Compton, who was Bishop of London from 1675 to 1713. As well as the trees and a fine rose garden there is a walled garden and a knot garden, both laid out as they would have been planted when they were created in the 19th century.

☞ After visiting Fulham Palace retrace your steps to Putney Bridge, cross back over the road, turn right and go over the bridge for . . .

ST MARY'S CHURCH, PUTNEY
Open daily • Free

There is not much on the outside to suggest that this pleasant but unspectacular church tucked up against the south side of Putney Bridge is a place of wonder and pilgrimage. But indeed it is, at least for all people who value the cherished rights and freedoms that we enjoy in Britain today. Here, for 12 days in 1647, while England was convulsed in Civil War and the king was being held captive, Oliver Cromwell and Henry Ireton, leaders of the all-conquering parliamentary army, met with a group of radical thinkers from the rank and file, later known as the Levellers, to debate the political future of England. Extraordinary concepts, such as 'one man one vote' and 'equality before the law for all', were aired and discussed openly for the first time and, indeed, an agreement of sorts was reached, but it was never followed up and the Putney Debates were quietly forgotten. But the ideas were now out there and became an inspiration and rallying cry for all the great civil rights campaigns that followed. Indeed, the civil rights first articulated at Putney were even enshrined in the American Constitution 130 years later.

St Mary's, Putney, now stands as a monument to the first stirrings of modern democracy and freedom across the world, and inside there is a superb exhibition that celebrates these Putney Debates, tells their story, and explains their significance in advancing the cause of civil liberties. The space inside is bright and cheerful with light flooding in through huge windows, and at the north-east end of the church there is a lovely 16th-century Chantry Chapel with a fan-vaulted ceiling, a miniature of the Chantry Chapel in Ely Cathedral given to the church by Bishop West of Ely. A truly inspirational place.

WALK TWO

SOUTHFIELDS

The home of tennis

WIMBLEDON LAWN TENNIS MUSEUM
15 minutes • Open daily • Charge

DIRECTIONS
Exit station, use the lights to your right to cross over Augustus Road and walk straight ahead on Wimbledon Park Road to the museum. On the way you may wish to cross over the road and enjoy the wide views over Wimbledon Park, with its huge ornamental lake, all that remains of the grounds of Wimbledon Manor, laid out by Capability Brown in the 18th century. During the 19th century Wimbledon Manor was one of the homes of the Earls Spencer, ancestors of Diana, Princess of Wales. Today it is a public park and golf course.

The All England Club moved to Church Road in Wimbledon from nearby Worple Road in 1922, since when it has been the home of the most famous tennis tournament – and the most famous tennis court, Centre Court – in the world. The Lawn Tennis Museum, which opened in 1977, is the world's largest museum of tennis and tells the story of the game's evolution from a knockabout in the garden to a world-wide sport played

by millions. On display there are exhibits and tennis memorabilia dating back as far as 1555, mementoes and trophies from
the very first championships in 1877 right up to those of the
present day, historic film footage of some of Wimbledon's most
memorable matches, and the tennis whites and tennis racquets
of famous players. More recent highlights include a 3D film
about life at Wimbledon, a 360-degree viewing platform overlooking the Centre Court and the ghost of John McEnroe
speaking from his dressing-room about his Wimbledon
experiences.

Along with the museum and regular temporary exhibitions visitors can (by appointment) browse in the Kenneth
Ritchie Wimbledon Library, the largest tennis library in the
world, and there are daily tours that take you behind the scenes
at Wimbledon with access to both Court No. 1 and Centre
Court.

West – Richmond Branch

WALK THREE

TURNHAM GREEN
Also served by Piccadilly Line

*One of the finest examples of neo-Palladian architecture in
Britain, an artist's summer residence, some noble tombs and
London's pride*

CHISWICK HOUSE

20 minutes • House open Sun-Wed; gardens daily
• House admission charge; gardens free

DIRECTIONS

Exit station, cross over and turn left. Go down to
Chiswick High Road, cross over using the lights to
your right and turn right in front of the shops. Turn
next left into Devonshire Road (or carry on for 50 yards
(45 m) to visit the celebrated Foster's Bookshop, which is
located in a charming 18th-century shop, the oldest
on Chiswick High Road, and sells an excellent range
of books, old and new). Go to the end of Devonshire
Road, enter the subway on your right and follow the
signs to Hogarth's House (*see* below). Go past
Hogarth's House, along Hogarth's Lane, for another 200
yards (180 m) until you see a brown sign pointing left
to Chiswick House. From here follow the signs through
Chiswick Gardens to the house.

One of Britain's Palladian treasures, Chiswick House was
designed and built by the 3rd Earl of Burlington between 1724
and 1729 as a 'temple to the arts', somewhere to display his
extensive collection of paintings and other works. The resplen-
dent interiors were created with the help of architect William
Kent. After Lord Burlington died in 1753 the house passed
to his daughter, wife of the 4th Duke of Devonshire, and the
Devonshire family kept possession until 1929. During that time
Chiswick House hosted many dazzling high society parties and
welcomed an array of famous guests including Voltaire, Jean-
Jacques Rousseau, US Presidents John Adams and Thomas

Jefferson, Benjamin Franklin, Tsars Nicolas I and Alexander I, Handel, Queen Victoria and many political figures. Foreign Secretary Charles James Fox died there in 1806, as did Prime Minister George Canning, in the same room, in 1827. Today, thanks to a massive effort after years of neglect, Chiswick House has been restored to its full glory, with Old Masters gracing the walls and the rooms filled with works of art and fine furniture such as the famous neo-Palladian Chiswick tables designed by Kent.

In the Green Velvet Room hangs a set of eight landscape views of the garden at Chiswick, commissioned by Lord Burlington from the Dutch artist Pieter Rysbrack. They record the development of the garden, which was laid out by William Kent and is considered to be the first English landscape garden. Covering 65 acres (26 ha) the garden includes a lake, cascades, a classical stone bridge, statues and temples, and a camellia collection in the conservatory that is the oldest collection of camellias under glass in the Western world.

In May 1966 the Beatles visited the grounds of Chiswick House to shoot the world's very first pop video, a promotional film for their double A-side single 'Paperback Writer' and 'Rain'.

HOGARTH'S HOUSE
15 minutes • Open Tues-Sun • Free

DIRECTIONS
Follow directions for Chiswick House and signs to Hogarth's House.

Now situated right beside the busy stretch of the Great West Road that is named after him, this lovely early 18th-century house was artist William Hogarth's summer residence for 15 years, somewhere he could come and get away from the noise and stress of his London house in Leicester Square and work in his 'painting room' at the bottom of the garden. In 1904 the house was opened as a museum of his life and works. William Hogarth was not just an artist and print-maker and one of our first cartoonists, but also a satirist and political commentator, and his pictures showing the seamier side of life in Georgian London led to him being described as 'the defining spirit of London's art'. The rooms of Hogarth's House are hung with a selection of his works and laid out as they would have been when he lived there, with replicas of his furniture based on pieces seen in the artist's prints. There is also a gallery in the kitchen wing reserved for temporary exhibitions. Outside in the walled garden is an ancient mulberry tree that provided fruit with which Hogarth and his wife made mulberry pies for the Foundling children they had to stay – Hogarth was a great supporter of Thomas Coram's newly opened Foundling School (*see* Russell Square, Piccadilly Line).

ST NICHOLAS CHURCH, CHISWICK
15 minutes • Open daily • Free

DIRECTIONS
Follow directions for Chiswick House but bear left in subway at the end of Devonshire Road and follow signs to Fuller's Brewery. As you emerge from subway bear right into Church Street. St Nicholas is at the end on the right.

The much restored 15th-century parish church of Chiswick sits by the River Thames at the end of a short street of fine Georgian houses, on the site of a Norman church. The ragstone tower is all that remains from the 15th century, the rest of the building dating from a restoration of 1882 paid for by brewer Henry Smith from the brewery next door (now Fuller's Brewery, *see* below).

William Hogarth is buried outside the south side of the church beneath a square stone pedestal topped with a stone urn. The tomb is engraved with a poem by the actor David Garrick. St Nicholas churchyard has a number of other notable residents too, their graves identified on a map available in the church. Amongst them are Lord Frederick Cavendish, who was Irish Secretary under William Gladstone, and was murdered by Fenians in Phoenix Park, Dublin; Oliver Cromwell's daughter, Mary Fauconberg; Henry Joy, the trumpeter who sounded the Charge of the Light Brigade; artist James McNeill Whistler, known for his painting *Whistler's Mother*; Charles II's mistress Barbara Villiers, whose children by the King were given the name Fitzroy; and Frederick Hitch, who won the VC at Rorke's Drift during the Anglo-Zulu War.

FULLER'S BREWERY
15 minutes • Open Mon-Fri • Pre-booked tours
only • Charge

DIRECTIONS
Follow directions for Chiswick House above and,
when you reach the subway, follow signs to
the brewery tour.

From St Nicholas Church go back up Church Street toward
the A4 and on your right is Fuller's Brewery, home of Fuller,
Smith and Turner PLC, brewers of London Pride. The Griffin
brewery, as it has been known since 1816, grew out of a small
private brewhouse set up in the back garden of Bedford House
on Chiswick Mall in the 17th century, and is now the biggest
brewery in London. Whatever they brew here must be effica-
cious, for growing up the wall of one of the brewery's Georgian
office buildings in the middle of the complex is the oldest wisteria
in Britain, one of two introduced into England in 1816. The
other one, which was planted at abstemious Kew, died. For the
hugely popular brewery tour (admission charge) follow the signs.

WALK FOUR

GUNNERSBURY
Also served by Overground

*A pair of uniquely fascinating museums where you can see
the world's largest working beam engine and hear a rare
Mighty Wurlitzer*

LONDON MUSEUM OF WATER & STEAM
15 minutes • Open daily • Charge

DIRECTIONS
Exit station, turn left and walk along Chiswick
High Road to the roundabout at the end. Using the
pedestrian crossings go to the centre of the roundabout
and take the pathway across the roundabout, bearing
slightly right under the M4, to the other side. The ESSO
station should be in front of you across the road slightly right.
Use the first crossing then the crossing on your right. Turn
left keeping the ESSO station on your right, and continue
along Chiswick High Road, past the Leisure Centre and Kew
Bridge station into Kew Bridge Road. Keeping right, head
for the tall standpipe tower that marks the
entrance to the museum.

Described as 'the most important historic
site of the water supply industry in
Britain', the London Museum of Water
& Steam was founded in 1975 and is
based in the old Kew Bridge Pumping
Station. The core of the museum is
its collection of historic 19th-century
steam engines that were used
for pumping water. It
is home to the world's
largest collection of
Cornish beam engines,
so called as they were
the type of engines

used to pump water out of the tin mines in Cornwall and to operate Cornwall's 'man lifts', an early type of elevator that conveyed miners up and down from the tunnels. The museum also houses the largest working beam engine in the world, the Grand Junction 90, which is 40 feet (12 m) high, weighs 250 tons and was used to pump water to London for 98 years. It was described by no less an admirer than Charles Dickens as 'a monster' and it is an amazing experience to see an engine of this vast size being steamed up, which it is regularly, as are most of the other engines. There is also a huge waterwheel, as used to pump water before the days of steam, a courtyard where you can try out different ways of moving water, a small-gauge steam railway and an interactive gallery that tells the story of London's water supply.

The buildings in which the museum is housed are as historic as the collection itself. The original engine house, which contains amongst its exhibits the only complete working Bull engine in the world, was built in 1837, while the Great Engine House, where the biggest engines are housed, was built between 1845 and 1869. But the most eye-catching structure is the 200 ft (61 m) high Italianate standpipe tower at the entrance. Built in 1867, this is a real west London landmark and a most effective way of locating the museum.

THE MUSICAL MUSEUM
18 minutes ● Open Friday, Saturday, Sunday ● Charge

DIRECTIONS
As for steam museum, then the Musical Museum is a little further along Kew Bridge Road on the right.

Founded by Frank Holland in 1963, the Musical Museum possesses one of the world's most important collections of self-playing musical instruments, including keyboards, strings, pipe organs and wind instruments, as well as early gramophones, juke boxes, music boxes and musical toys. Originally housed in St George's Church just down the road, in 2003 the museum moved to its present purpose-built home where there is a 200-seat auditorium for concerts, films, exhibitions and demonstrations. There are regular guided tours of the museum (11.30am, 1.30pm and 3.30pm) during which the guide will play many of the instruments – the highlight being a performance on the museum's vintage 1930s Hammond organ or on the lovingly restored 'Mighty Wurlitzer'. There are very few of these magnificent instruments that survive. This one at the Musical Museum once thrilled audiences at the Kingston Regal, providing the sound track and effects for silent movies and later, after the introduction of 'talkies', being used for entertainment during the interval.

WALK FIVE

KEW GARDENS

The world's most famous garden

KEW GARDENS
Open daily • Charge

DIRECTIONS
Follow signs from the station.

Covering some 300 acres (121 ha), Kew Gardens is home to the world's largest collection of living plants, to one of the world's largest herbariums, containing over seven million specimens, and to 14,000 trees from more than 2,000 different species. The story of Kew Gardens begins in the early 18th century when Prince George (later George II) and his wife Caroline started a garden on their estate beside the River Thames at Kew. In the 1730s their son Frederick, Prince of Wales, acquired an adjacent estate where he began landscaping his own garden. Prince Frederick died in 1751 but his widow, Princess Augusta, carried on with the garden at Kew and in 1759 set up a botanic garden there. The two gardens were eventually merged by George III into what is now Kew Gardens – which is why it is Kew 'Gardens' and not Kew 'Garden'. George III handed over the running of the combined gardens to Sir Joseph Banks, and it was under his guidance that the gardens developed into the world-famous institution of today. Banks not only donated his own vast collection of plants, gathered on his voyages around the world with Captain Cook, but encouraged and organised others to seek out new species from all over the planet and bring them back to Kew where they could be studied. In 1840 the gardens were taken over by the nation and became a key centre for scientific and botanical research at the heart of the burgeoning British Empire.

Highlights include the first ginkgo tree ever planted in Britain, a pinetum, a lake, riverside walks, an 18th-century pagoda, the oldest pot plant in the world, the largest surviving Victorian glasshouse in the world, a palm house, a treetop walkway, a royal palace where Queen Victoria's parents were married and a huge variety of specialist gardens, greenhouses and woodlands.

East from Earl's Court

WALK SIX

ALDGATE EAST
Also served by Hammersmith & City Line

Anarchy, public art and Britain's oldest manufacturing company

FREEDOM PRESS

DIRECTIONS
As you come out of the station turn right, go past the Whitechapel Gallery, and on your right next to Kentucky Fried Chicken is the entrance to Angel Alley.

This is the home of Freedom Press, the biggest anarchist publishing house in Britain and the oldest such organisation in the world. It was founded in 1886 by Cambridge-educated anarchist writer Charlotte Wilson and Russian philosopher Peter Kropotkin, who together founded *Freedom*, until recently the UK's only regularly published national anarchist newspaper – it has now moved online. Hidden away down the alley, beside a mural depicting Leo Tolstoy, Noam Chomsky and Emiliano Zapata, is the Freedom Press bookshop where you can browse through works such as *Anarchy in Action*, *Anarchists Against Bombs*, *Why Work? Arguments for the Leisure Society*, and the *Anarchist Quiz Book*.

WHITECHAPEL GALLERY
Open Tues-Sun • Free

DIRECTIONS
As you exit the station, next door on your right.

Founded in 1901 with the intention of making art accessible to the people of the East End and providing a showcase for local talent, the Whitechapel Gallery was one of the first publicly funded galleries in London and has developed into one of London's most influential art and exhibition venues. The event that really put the gallery on the map took place in 1939 when it was chosen to exhibit Picasso's *Guernica*, painted as a protest against the bombing of the Spanish village of that name by Nationalist forces during the Spanish Civil War. Since then the gallery has premiered many international masters, Jackson Pollock and Mark Rothko to mention just two, as well as putting on the first major retrospectives of David Hockney and German sculptor Isa Genzken. It has also championed established British artists, such as Gilbert & George, Lucian Freud and Bridget Riley, and contemporary artists, including Sophie Calle and Mark Wallinger.

WHITECHAPEL BELL FOUNDRY
Open Mon-Fri ● Museum free – pre-booked tours charge

DIRECTIONS
Exit station and turn left along Whitechapel Road.
The foundry is 300 yards (270 m) along on the other
side of the road.

The bells, the bells . . . Occupying some of the oldest buildings in Whitechapel, which were built in 1670 just after the Great Fire,

Britain's oldest manufacturing company has had a presence in the East End since the reign of Henry V, and has occupied the premises here since 1728. Here, in 1752, was cast the Liberty Bell, commissioned to celebrate the 50th anniversary of William Penn's 1701 Charter of Privileges, the original constitution of Pennsylvania, and rung from the steeple of the Philadelphia State House in 1776 to acclaim the first reading of the American Declaration of Independence there. Here, in 1858, was cast Big Ben, the hour bell for the Great Clock of Westminster, the largest bell ever cast at Whitechapel and the most famous, and most listened to, bell in the world. Bells have gone out from here to St Petersburg, Washington, Toronto, Birmingham and many other far-flung places. Here were cast Lincoln Cathedral's Great Tom, audible from 13 miles (21 km) away, the bells of Westminster Abbey, and the 13 bells of Liverpool's Anglican cathedral, the heaviest peal of bells in the world. A tour of this historic site is fascinating. There is also a small museum in the foyer (admission free) and a foundry store selling bells and other bell-related merchandise.

WALK SEVEN

WHITECHAPEL
Also served by Hammersmith & City and Overground Lines

ROYAL LONDON HOSPITAL MUSEUM
Open Tues-Fri • Free

DIRECTIONS
Straight across the road from the station.

Located in the crypt of 19th-century St Philip's Church in the grounds of the Royal London Hospital, which was founded in 1740 and was at one time the largest voluntary hospital in Britain, this museum covers the history of medicine in the East End and more specifically of the Royal London. Exhibits include historic surgical instruments, medical and nursing equipment, and an operations bell of 1792, rung to summon attendants to hold patients down during an operation before the days of anaesthetics. There is also some particularly fascinating material related to a number of the hospital's more celebrated characters, such as Dr Barnardo, who studied here at the medical school and was moved to set up his ragged school in nearby Stepney; Joseph Merrick, the Elephant Man, who lived out his life in a private room in the hospital; and nurse Edith Cavell, executed for helping Allied soldiers to escape from Belgium during the First World War.

WALK EIGHT

BROMLEY-BY-BOW

Also served by Hammersmith & City Line

The world's largest tidal mills

THREE MILLS ISLAND
DIRECTIONS

Exit station, go down steps to your left and right through underpass. Climb steps to road level and turn right going downhill against the traffic. After 100 yards (90 m) bear right at slip road and continue, keeping Tesco on

your right. At the end of Tesco turn right into
Three Mills Lane. The mills are straight ahead.

The Domesday Book of 1086 records eight mills here on
the River Lea, meaning that Three Mills Island is the site of
Britain's earliest recorded tidal mill system. Today it is a beautiful riverside oasis of cobbles and Georgian splendour in the
gritty East End, and home to the oldest tidal mill in Britain,
which is also the largest tidal mill in the world.

THE HOUSE MILL
Open Sundays in summer months • Guided tours
only – charge

The House Mill was built in 1776 by Daniel Bisson on the site
of an earlier mill and rebuilt a few years later after a fire. Initially
used to produce flour, in 1872 the mill was bought by gin distillers
J.&W. Nicholson and was operated as part of a distillery.
Gin production stopped during the Second World War due
to rationing, and because the area was badly bombed the mill
ceased operating altogether in 1941. It has since been lovingly

restored and retains much of its original machinery, including the four mill wheels and six of the twelve pairs of millstones. The name House Mill comes from the fact that it stood between two houses that were lived in by the miller and his family. The Miller's House next door was damaged in the 1941 bombing but was later rebuilt behind the original Georgian façade, which bears the date 1776 alongside Daniel Bisson's initials. There is a café and gallery space here as well as a small information centre with leaflets about walks along the various local waterways.

Next door again is the Clock Mill, built in 1815, and incorporating a clock from the previous mill. The clock mill continued in operation until 1952. The third of the three mills was a windmill, which was demolished in 1840.

The Clock Mill and the rest of Three Mills Island is now occupied by one of London's largest film and television studios, 3 Mills Studios. This was the site of the original Big Brother House and is where film director Danny Boyle was based while planning the Opening Ceremony for the 2012 Olympic Games.

The House Mill is open for guided tours on Sundays in summer only, but Three Mills Island is a most beautiful and interesting place to visit at any time, and the pleasant Miller's House Café is open daily.

WALK NINE

BARKING

Also served by Hammersmith & City and Overground Lines

Romantic remains of the first nunnery in England

BARKING ABBEY
Open daily (Curfew Tower open Weds) • Free

DIRECTIONS
Exit station and turn right. Walk straight ahead and
carry on along the pedestrianised street, lined with
shops and market stalls, until the end. You will
see Abbey Green ahead of you across North Street.

In 661 Bishop Erkenwald of London, who was of royal
ancestry, founded two abbeys, one at Chertsey for men and
this one at Barking for women, the first nunnery in England.
Erkenwald's sister Ethelburg became the first abbess and from
that time until the abbey was dissolved in 1539 the Abbess of
Barking held precedence over all other abbesses in England.
Despite losing much of its land to floods in 1377 the abbey was
for most of its existence one of the richest and most powerful
in the country and played host to many important characters
in England's history. William the Conqueror stayed at the
abbey while the Tower of London was being built; Henry II
made Thomas Becket's sister, Mary, the Abbess of Barking in
reparation for her brother's murder in Canterbury Cathedral;
Chaucer's sister, Elizabeth, became a nun at Barking in 1381;
and Edmund and Jasper Tudor, the children of Owen Tudor
and Henry V's widow Catherine de Valois, were educated
there. Edmund would go on to father Henry VII, founder
of the Tudor royal dynasty. Ironically, Edmund's grandson,
Henry VIII, was responsible for the abbey's destruction during
the Dissolution of the Monasteries in 1539.

Substantial parts of the abbey walls are still standing, to a
height of several feet, and the footprint and foundations are clearly

visible, but the only part of the abbey still complete is the Curfew Tower of 1370. One of the abbey's greatest treasures, which drew many pilgrims to Barking, can be found in the Chapel of the Holy Rood above the arch of the Curfew Tower: a rare 12th-century stone rood, one of only four or five in Britain, set in the east wall. The tower is open on some Wednesdays, admission free.

St Margaret's Church, inside the abbey grounds, is largely 13th-century but shows signs of Saxon and Norman work from an earlier chapel, and the whitewashed interior is worth a look. Captain Cook was married here, to Elizabeth Batts, in 1762. There is a small museum of local history at the back of the church.

The church and abbey ruins are contained in a pleasant park called Abbey Green, a welcome respite from the bustle of Barking.

WALK TEN

UPNEY

Unspoiled Elizabethan red-brick manor house in an unlikely setting

EASTBURY MANOR

● Open Weds, Thurs and Sun ● Charge ● National Trust

DIRECTIONS

Exit station and turn right. Carry on down to the traffic lights at the end of the road. Cross over the main road at the lights on your right and go straight ahead through bollards

into Blake Avenue. Turn first right down Sisley Road and
Eastbury Manor is on the left after 100 yards (90 m).

Now hemmed in by acres of housing estate, this impressive
Tudor mansion once stood on an isolated patch of ground
raised above the surrounding marshes, with views south to the
Thames. It was built in 1573 for a prosperous City merchant
called Clement Sysley on land that had become available after
the dissolution of Barking Abbey. Although it has lost one
of its great turret staircases, the house has been little altered
outside, as much due to neglect as anything else, and is a fine
example of Elizabethan architecture.

For the first hundred years or so the house was occupied by
families of the gentry, including John Moore, stepfather-in-law
of Lewis Tresham, brother of the Francis Tresham involved in

the Gunpowder Plot. Local legend suggests that events related to the plot may have taken place in Eastbury Manor. During the 18th and 19th centuries the house was lived in by tenants and allowed to run down until bought by the National Trust in 1918.

Highlights include a Great Chamber with impressive 17th-century wall paintings, a magnificent exposed wooden roof in the attic above, an original oak spiral staircase, fine Tudor chimneys and a walled garden with special niches for beehives.

CHAPTER FIVE

The Hammersmith & City Line

. . . if you wish to have a just notion of the magnitude of this city, you must not be satisfied with seeing its great streets and squares, but must survey the innumerable little lanes and courts

Dr Johnson

COLOUR: PINK

YEAR OPENED AS A SEPARATE LINE: 1990

LENGTH: 15.8 MILES

FASCINATING FACT:

HAMMERSMITH & CITY LINE IS TECHNICALLY LONDON'S NEWEST TUBE LINE AS IT WAS ONLY SHOWN AS A SEPARATE LINE IN 1990. IT ALSO INCLUDES LONDON UNDERGROUND'S NEWEST STATION (WOOD LANE) AND THE LAST STATION TO CHANGE ITS NAME, SHEPHERD'S BUSH TO SHEPHERD'S BUSH MARKET IN 2008

WALK ONE

LADBROKE GROVE
Also served by Circle Line

MUSEUM OF BRANDS, PACKAGING AND ADVERTISING
Open Tues-Sun • Charge

DIRECTIONS
Exit station, turn right and right again into
Lancaster Road. The museum is 200 yards
(180 m) along on your left.

More or less as it says on the tin, this museum is all about brands, packaging and advertising, from Victorian days to the present, and explores how packaging reflects the culture and the events of its time, from the suffragettes to wartime rationing, from the days of the corner shop to the era of supermarkets, from royal marriages to golden jubilees – royalty was always a great selling point. Most of the items are products that we have become so familiar with that we hardly notice them, and yet many of the packages and logos are brilliant works of art, so cleverly designed that we can recognise them instantly. The museum promises 'ten thousand memories' and one of the great joys of coming here is nostalgia – you cannot help but squeal with delight on recognising some long-forgotten product from your childhood that brings the memories flooding back. In my case it was the Aztec bar – I was allowed to share one with my dad on Sunday afternoons. I hadn't even realised they were gone, but I was instantly transported back to the smell of the Balkan Sobranie he smoked in his pipe, *The Clitheroe Kid* on the radio and the Triumph Herald in the drive – who knew that packaging could be so evocative? Everyone will have their own favourite.

The museum was started in Gloucester in 1984 by Robert Opie, who was eating a packet of Munchies while standing waiting for a train, and instead of throwing the empty packaging away he decided to keep it as a memento. The collection kept growing and eventually it was moved to a Notting Hill mews in 2005 and then to the London Lighthouse Building in Lancaster Road in 2015.

There are some 12,000 items displayed chronologically in a 'time tunnel' that takes you through the changing faces of packaging and advertising, everything from foodstuffs, chocolate bars and sweets to washing powders, record sleeves, comics, a chopper bike, radios, toys, models, book covers, bottles, beer cans – it has to be the most colourful museum in London and one of the most fun.

WALK TWO

EUSTON SQUARE

Also served by Metropolitan and Circle Lines

Magic, medicine, a sculpture show, a 183-year-old man, an extinct zebra, Egyptian artefacts and the biggest church you never knew about

THE MAGIC CIRCLE MUSEUM
Regular open days and guided tours • Free

DIRECTIONS
Use Euston Road North Side exit. Turn right, and
right up North Gower Street and immediately right into
Stephenson Way. Club is on the left under a blue awning.

Tucked away down a narrow cobbled street near Euston station
is the headquarters of the Magic Circle, founded in 1905 by a
small group of magicians keen to create an association where
they could share ideas and tricks while keeping their secrets safe.
The name Magic Circle shares the initials of one of those who
came up with the idea, the young Martin Chapender, who died
too young at just 25. There are now some 1,500 members of the
Magic Circle from 38 countries, and amongst the membership
are such luminaries as the Prince of Wales, David Copperfield,
Ken Dodd and racing driver Nigel Mansell.

The very first official meeting of the Magic Circle was held
at the Green Man pub in Soho. After that the Circle met at a
number of performance venues before coming to rest at their
purpose-built headquarters in Stephenson Way in 1998. The
interior of the building is magnificent, with a theatre, museum
and members' library of some 10,000 books, as well as reception
rooms and a dining room and bar that are available for corpo-
rate hire and events.

The Magic Circle Museum is dedicated to the history of magic
and contains a unique collection of records, photographs, artefacts and magic paraphernalia. Highlights include Houdini's hand-
cuffs and a recording of his voice taken from an Edison cylinder
phonograph; items belonging to Jean Eugène Robert-Houdin, the

French magician considered the father of modern magic (and from whom Houdini took his name); the rifles used in Maurice Fogel's 'bullet catch' trick from the 1940s and the robes worn by Chung Ling Soo, who died when the bullet catch trick went wrong in 1918; props used by TV's comic magician Tommy Cooper; and the famous Zig Zag Lady illusion invented by Robert Harbin, whereby the assistant is carved into thirds. And did the British army use magic to hide the Suez Canal from German bombers in the Second World War? Find out here.

The museum is not open to the casual visitor but there is a constant programme of shows, guided tours and open days that provide access to it. Admission to the museum is free.

WELLCOME COLLECTION
Open Tues-Sun • Free

DIRECTIONS
Use Euston Road South Side exit, turn right along
Euston Road and the collection is on the right after
100 yards (90 m).

Advertised as 'the free visitor destination for the incurably curious', the Wellcome Collection is a unique museum of medicines and medical equipment that displays medical artefacts and curios from around the world and explores the science of healing through the connections between medicine, life and art.

There are frequent exhibitions, a vast library and two permanent galleries: Medicine Man, displaying articles from founder Henry Wellcome's own collection, including items belonging to Edward Jenner, the pioneer of vaccination, and articles from the laboratory of Joseph Lister, the pioneer of antiseptic surgery and hygiene; and Medicine Now, which uses modern media displays and objects to present aspects of medicine today.

The Wellcome Collection is part of the Wellcome Trust, a global charitable foundation dedicated to improvements in human and animal health worldwide, and the world's second largest private funding organisation after the Bill Gates Foundation. It was founded in 1936 with legacies bequeathed by pharmacist Sir Henry Wellcome, whose company Burroughs Wellcome & Co. was the first to introduce medicine in tablet form as opposed to powder or liquid, and who in 1902 opened the world's first research laboratory for tropical diseases, in Khartoum.

The Wellcome Collection, and the public functions of the Wellcome Trust, are housed in the original Wellcome Building on Euston Road, which was built in 1932 to the exact specifications of Sir Henry Wellcome. In 2004 the offices of the Wellcome Trust moved next door to a spectacular purpose-built glass edifice known as the Gibbs Building, which incorporates an entrance to Euston Square underground station.

UNIVERSITY COLLEGE LONDON

Euston Square underground station (Euston Road South Side exit) sits at the north end of Gower Street, which is dominated by the campus buildings of University College London (UCL), founded in 1826 as London University and the first university in England to admit students regardless of religion or gender. Hidden away in various corners of the campus are a number of fascinating museums and collections well worth seeking out. The main entrance to the campus is in Gower Street, about

100 yards (90 m) from the station entrance (turn left on exit) and from there signs can direct you to each attraction, or you can download a map at www.ucl.ac.uk/maps.

FLAXMAN GALLERY
Open daily • Free

The Flaxman Gallery, located in the main library under the university's dome at the main entrance, showcases works, prints and plaster models by the sculptor John Flaxman. Born in 1755 in York, John Flaxman was the leading British sculptor of his day and was particularly admired for his memorial sculptures, many of which can be seen in churches and cathedrals up and down the country. He died in 1826, the year that UCL was founded, and his studio collection was bought for the university by his old friend and College Council member Henry Crabb Robinson and placed on display under the UCL dome in 1851, where it was much admired by Prince Albert. Although many pieces were lost to bombing in the Second World War, the collection is still the largest existing collection of Flaxman's work and presents a splendid ensemble gathered around a full-scale model of St Michael overcoming Satan.

JEREMY BENTHAM AUTO-ICON
Open daily • Free

One of London's more bizarre attractions is the philosopher and reformer Jeremy Bentham, who sits in a glass-fronted wooden cabinet at the end of the south cloisters of UCL's main building. A noted liberal thinker and the founder of utilitarianism, he was an early advocate for animal rights and universal suffrage as well as the abolition of slavery and of the death penalty.

In a will made some 60 years before his death in 1832 he declared that he wanted his body dissected and then preserved as an 'auto-icon', and here he is, keen and eerily realistic. His skeleton, padded out with straw, dressed in his own clothes and topped with a wax head garnished with his real hair, has sat here since 1850, gazing out at generations of students and gawpers, always civil, always urbane. He originally intended that his real head should be used, but the mummification process left it looking rather too shrunken and macabre, and so it was placed at his feet and the wax head substituted.

In 1975 Bentham's head was stolen by students from King's College but returned after a ransom payment of £10 to Shelter. Not long afterwards it was removed from the cabinet and is now kept in a special environment in UCL's Institute of Archaeology, where it can be viewed by appointment.

In 1976 Jeremy Bentham attended the 150th anniversary of the founding of UCL (of which he is considered the spiritual founder) and he is occasionally invited to special events, most recently in April 2006 when he was guest of honour at a dinner during the John Stuart Mill Bicentennial Conference held at the university – John Stuart Mill had been Bentham's student.

GRANT MUSEUM OF ZOOLOGY
Open Mon-Sat afternoons • Free

DIRECTIONS
Just across Gower Street from main UCL entrance.

Founded in 1828 by UCL's Professor of Comparative Anatomy, Robert Grant, for teaching and dissection purposes, the Grant Museum of Zoology contains some 67,000 zoological specimens covering the entire animal kingdom. Here there are rows of bones and skeletons, mounted and hanging or just lying there, along with specimens preserved in fluid and a large collection of insects. Highlights include the bones of a dodo, extinct since 1681, a large jar of perfectly preserved moles, a selection of brains, a snake skeleton wrapped around a branch from London Zoo, a number of bisected animal heads and the rarest skeleton in the world, a type of South African zebra called a quagga, extinct since 1883 – this is one of only seven known examples.

PETRIE MUSEUM OF EGYPTIAN ARCHAEOLOGY
Open Tues-Sat afternoons • Free

DIRECTIONS
From UCL main entrance turn left and go south on Gower Street. Take first left into Torrington Place and go left through iron gates into Malet Place.

The Petrie Museum houses some 80,000 Egyptian and Sudanese objects, including tiles, carvings, frescoes, jewellery, tools, weapons, stone vessels, weights and measures, all illustrating life in the Nile Valley from prehistory to the Islamic era of the 16th century. It was established in 1892 thanks to a bequest from the writer Amelia Edwards, and the collection was greatly enlarged with the acquisition of objects and antiquities excavated in Egypt by Flinders Petrie, UCL's first Edwards Professor of Egyptian Archaeology and Philology. Because the removal of antiquities from Egypt and the Sudan is now banned, the Petrie Collection is one of the largest collections of Egyptian antiquities outside Egypt. Highlights include the world's largest collection of Roman period mummy portraits, iron beads that form the earliest example of Egyptian metalwork, the earliest piece of Egyptian linen, dated to 5000 BC, the oldest wills written on papyrus paper ever found, the only ancient Egyptian veterinary papyrus, a unique dancer's beadnet dress from 2400 BC and a suit of armour from the palace at Memphis.

CHURCH OF CHRIST THE KING
DIRECTIONS
Use Euston Road South Side exit, turn left down
Gower Street, first left into Torrington Place and church
is on the left after 200 yards (180 m).

A hidden gem, this church tucked up against the UCL buildings at the south-west corner of Gordon Square is often overlooked, but is one of the finest examples of Gothic Revival in Britain. Opened on Christmas Eve 1853, it was designed by J. Raphael Brandon and financed by the banker Henry Drummond for the Catholic Apostolic Church, of which he was a founder. It is a Westminster Abbey in miniature, with the second highest nave in England (the Abbey has the highest) but unfortunately the glorious interior can only be glimpsed from a lobby area beside the Cloisters, reached through an arched doorway off Gordon Square. Having been the UCL church, Christ the King is now home to the Forward in Faith movement and is open to the public for a weekly mass or for the occasional organ recital.

We can but hope that this may change, for such a magnificent church deserves to be seen.

WALK THREE

KING'S CROSS ST PANCRAS

Also served by Metropolitan, Circle, Northern, Piccadilly and Victoria Lines

The biggest interchange station on the Tube network, served by more underground lines than any other station. Both main-line stations here are of interest in their own right.

KING'S CROSS RAILWAY STATION

King's Cross is the site of one of the largest regeneration schemes in Europe, where 67 acres (27 ha) of brownfield land is being developed into homes, shops and offices, including the new headquarters of Google UK. King's Cross station, famous from the Monopoly board, has also undergone major redevelopment, with the original Victorian façade of 1852 revealed and a new departures concourse opened in 2012, covered by a steel roof making it the largest single-span structure in Europe.

King's Cross gets its name from a statue of George IV erected nearby in 1830 at what was then called Battle Bridge crossroads and demolished in 1842. The name Battle Bridge recalls a battle thought to have been fought here between Britain's warrior queen Boudicca and the Romans. Boudicca was defeated and is said to be buried beneath Platform 9 or 10.

Boudicca's namesake Queen Victoria (Boudicca means victory) was one of the first passengers to leave from King's Cross when she took the train to Scotland from here in 1851.

Platform 9¾, from where the Hogwarts Express departs in the Harry Potter stories, can be found in the new western concourse. A cast-iron 'Platform 9¾' sign and the back half of a luggage trolley disappearing into the brick wall mark the spot, and on most days a queue of excited Harry Potter fans can be seen winding around the concourse as they await their turn to run at the wall with a trolley. Were they to succeed in breaching the wall they would find themselves in the superb Watermark Books, the first Watermark bookshop to open in Europe.

ST PANCRAS RAILWAY STATION AND HOTEL

Opened in 1868 as the London terminus of the Midland Railway, the rail shed of St Pancras station was at the time the largest single-span structure ever built. Between 2004 and 2007 the station was superbly restored and the glorious curved glass roof is now one of the sights of London. In 2007 the new St Pancras was opened by the Queen as the home of Eurostar trains to the Continent via the Channel Tunnel.

Fronting the station is one of Britain's most spectacular Victorian masterpieces, the former Midland Grand Hotel, built by George Gilbert Scott in 1873. The Midland Grand was one of the most luxurious hotels in Europe, boasting flushing lavatories, the first hotel lifts, the first room in Europe where women were allowed to smoke in public, Britain's first revolving door, fitted in 1899, and a Grand Staircase (where the Spice Girls made their first video 'Wannabe' in 1996).

Threatened with demolition in the 1960s, the building was saved by a campaign led by poet John Betjeman and there is a statue in his honour on the upper level of the station concourse. The hotel reopened as the St Pancras Renaissance London Hotel in 2011.

LONDON CANAL MUSEUM
Open Tues-Sun • Charge

DIRECTIONS
Take main exit from mainline station and turn left and left again up York Way. Take the third right at the traffic lights into Wharfedale Road. After 100 yards (90 m) turn left into New Wharf Road and museum is on the left.

Located beside the Grand Union Canal to the north of King's Cross station, the museum covers all aspects of London's canals and the UK's inland waterways: their history, how they were built, the lock system, the types of boats used, cargoes carried and the people (and horses) who worked and still work on them.

The museum opened in 1992 and is housed in a Victorian ice warehouse formerly used by Carlo Gatti, the Swiss entrepreneur who introduced both cafés and ice cream to the British public. The warehouse was built to store ice imported from Norway and delivered by ship and canal barge. The ice, which was sold to fishmongers and others who needed to keep food chilled, was kept in specially dug ice wells, one of which can be seen at the museum.

There are regular exhibitions, evening talks, organised walks along the towpath to Camden Town, and guided trips through the Islington Tunnel, built in 1818 to carry the Grand Union Canal for three-quarters of a mile (1.2 km) underneath Islington.

BRITISH LIBRARY
Open daily • Free

DIRECTIONS
Take main exit from mainline station and turn
right up Euston Road. The library is just past
St Pancras station on the right.

Since 1997 this has been the home of the biggest library collection in the world, with some 170 million items, both print and digital, books, manuscripts, journals, videos, recordings, maps, scripts, prints, drawings and more. The British Library is a copyright library, entitled to receive automatically a free copy of every item published or distributed in Britain.

A reader's pass is required for those wishing to use the reading rooms, but anyone can visit the exhibition galleries, where there are permanent displays and frequent themed exhibitions on such subjects as maps, sacred texts, Magna Carta and the history of the English language.

Highlights on display in the Sir John Ritblat Gallery include the 4th-century Codex Sinaiticus, written in Greek and one of the two earliest Christian Bibles; the Lindisfarne Gospels from the early 8th century; the world's oldest printed book, the Diamond Sutra, a sacred work of the Buddhist faith dated to 868; a unique manuscript of *Beowulf* in Old English from the 10th century; Gutenburg's 1455 Bible; Leonardo Da Vinci's notebook; Shakespeare's First Folio and Handel's *Messiah* written in the composer's own hand.

WALK FOUR

BARBICAN

Also served by Metropolitan and Circle Lines

A SHORT CIRCULAR WALK FROM BARBICAN STATION

☞ Exit station and turn left then next left into Carthusian Street. After 100 yards (90 m) turn right into Charterhouse Square and walk to the Charterhouse on the far side, passing the art deco Florin Court on your right. This was the residence of Hercule Poirot as played by David Suchet in the ITV television series *Poirot*.

THE CHARTERHOUSE
Pre-booked tours only until autumn 2016 • Charge

A medley of historic buildings on the site of a Carthusian monastery founded in 1371 beside a huge burial pit for victims of the Black Death. Charterhouse is an English corruption of the French name Chartreuse, a mountain range in south-east France from which both the Carthusian Order and the delicious green liqueur, get their name. After the Dissolution of the Monasteries the Charterhouse complex was transformed into a palatial residence by Sir Edward North and then the Duke of Norfolk, with a magnificent Great Hall and a Great Chamber where both Elizabeth I and James I held their first

Courts. Although restored after being bombed in the Second World War, these are still two of the finest Elizabethan rooms in London. In 1611 the house was purchased by coal merchant Thomas Sutton, the wealthiest commoner in England, who endowed a hospital on the site and left money for a school, a chapel in which he is buried, and almshouses for 80 'Brothers'. These were 'either decrepit or old captaynes either at sea or land, maimed or disabled soldiers, merchants fallen on hard times'. The school moved to Godalming in Surrey in 1872 but the Brothers remain *in situ* and eat all their meals together in the Great Hall.

Some of the early rules of football were established here while the Charterhouse was occupied by the school. The boys would play in the enclosed cloisters and when the ball went out of one of the window openings, if it could still be touched by a boy leaning out of the window, it would remain in play. Otherwise play would stop and one of the players would climb out of the window and throw the ball back into the cloister – hence the 'touch' line and the 'throw in'.

The Charterhouse is building a new visitor centre, which is to be run by the Museum of London and is due to open in the autumn of 2016.

☞ Exit Charterhouse, cross the square and turn right to . . .

Smithfield Market. The largest wholesale meat market in the UK, covering some 10 acres (4 ha), and the only significant wholesale market left in the City. Smithfield, or Smooth Field, was a large expanse of grass outside the city walls, good for grazing cattle, and became established as the site of London's livestock market well over 1,000 years ago. In 1123

St Bartholomew's Priory was founded to the east and the friars from there set up Bartholomew's Fair, London's biggest summer fair, held annually on Smithfield for over 700 years until it got too rowdy and was closed down in 1855. The field was also used for tournaments and jousts and as a place of execution. The Scottish nationalist William Wallace was executed here in 1305. In 1381, during the Peasants' Revolt, Richard II met the peasants' leader Wat Tyler here – after a short exchange of insults Tyler was killed by the Lord Mayor of London. The first formal cattle market was established in 1638 and rapidly grew into a huge enterprise with cattle being driven here from as far away as Scotland. There were frequent stampedes with terrified cattle ending up seeking refuge in houses and shops – the origin of the phrase 'a bull in a china shop'. Smithfield is now perhaps the most modern city-centre meat market in the world.

☞ Turn left through the market's Grand Avenue and you will come to a large roundabout beyond which is . . .

ST BARTHOLOMEW'S HOSPITAL MUSEUM
Open Tues-Fri • Free

DIRECTIONS
Enter through the Henry VIII gate on Giltspur
Street and go to the left under the
North Wing archway.

'Barts' is the oldest hospital in Europe. It was founded in 1123, along with the priory of St Bartholomew, by Rahere, a courtier to Henry I, who was inspired by a vision of St Bartholomew that came to him while he was sick on a pilgrimage to Rome. The hospital was refounded by Henry VIII in 1546 after the dissolution of the priory and there is a statue to Henry above the fine Palladian gateway of 1702, the only outdoor statue of Henry VIII in London. The walls of the grand staircase in the entrance hall to the hospital are decorated with murals by William Hogarth, who was born nearby and christened in the next-door church of St Bartholomew the Great. He painted the murals for free, to prove that an English artist could paint in the grand style, and modelled the sick and injured people in the painting on patients at the hospital – a hospital tradition says that novice doctors were sometimes tested on what they thought was wrong with each figure. The murals can be seen from the hospital museum in the north wing, where you can learn about the story of Barts and see facsimiles of Rahere's grant of 1137 and of the refounding agreement between Henry VIII and the City of London. There are also displays of historic medical instruments and a feature on William Harvey, who discovered the circulation of the blood and was physician at Barts for over 30 years from 1609 to 1643.

Just inside the Henry VIII gate, and often overlooked, is the church of **St Bartholomew the Less.** Built as a priory chapel in 1184, now the parish church of St Bartholomew's Hospital, and unique in being a parish in its own right, St Bartholomew the Less is so called to distinguish it from the Priory Church of St Bartholomew the Great next door (*see* below). The tower of the present building is 15th century, while the octagonal interior was created within the shell of the old church by George Dance the Younger in 1793. It is open daily.

Exit from the Henry VIII gate and turn left to see the Golden Boy, set high up on the wall of the red-and-white building at the corner of Giltspur Street and Cock Lane. He marks the furthest extent of the Great Fire of London in 1666 and was made prodigiously fat to act as a warning against gluttony, the sin to which the fire was attributed – it did, after all, begin in Pudding Lane.

☞ Turn round and walk back past the hospital gateway. In front of you is a 13th-century gateway surmounted by a 15th-century half-timbered chamber where Mary I sat drinking wine and eating chicken while Protestant martyrs were being burned alive outside. Go through the gateway to see the only surviving building from the 12th-century priory.

The Priory Church of St Bartholomew the Great, London's oldest surviving parish church. The interior, with its beautifully sinuous apse of round arches and round pillars, was described by John Betjeman as 'the finest Norman interior in London', and has been used many times as a film set – most memorably in *Four Weddings and a Funeral* and *Shakespeare in Love*. A highlight, and unique in London, is the 16th-century oriel window high on the south wall from where the prior could keep an eye on the monks below.

Shamefully, in 2007 St Bartholomew the Great became the first Anglican parish church in the country to charge an entrance fee.

☞ Return to Smithfield, turn left into Little Britain, third left into Montague Street and follow signs to ...

MUSEUM OF LONDON
Open daily • Free

One of the very best museums to be found anywhere, the Museum of London documents the history of London and its inhabitants from prehistory to the present day. Bringing together the collections of the Guildhall Museum and the London Museum, it was established in 1976 in these purpose-built premises as part of the new Barbican development. Arranged in interactive chronological galleries, highlights include a superb Roman mosaic found near Queen Victoria Street, a silk dress woven in Spitalfields by French Huguenots, a re-creation of an 18th-century pleasure garden, an original art deco lift from Selfridges and the Lord Mayor's State Coach.

The Museum of London is hoping to move to a new home in Smithfield Market in 2012.

☞ Exit the museum for ...

THE BARBICAN

Named after a long-gone watch-tower on the city walls, the Barbican estate was built over ten years between 1965 and 1975 on 35 acres (14 ha) of bombed-out land as a traffic-free residential complex with homes for 6,500 people, shops, schools, a museum and an arts centre. Concrete and brutalist, it is redolent of its era, which is presumably why it is Grade II listed. The three Barbican towers are over 400 feet (120 m) high and were the tallest residential towers in Europe when they were built. A maze of elevated walkways link the various amenities, which are grouped around garden squares and a lake. Apparently, there are over 100 ways of entering the Barbican, and it's easy to lose your bearings, but a gentle walk around the estate yields unexpected delights, such as stretches of Roman wall, fountains, flower gardens and monuments. Right in the middle of the complex, beside a bastion of the old wall and marooned in a sea of 1960s concrete, is one of the few surviving medieval churches in the City.

St Giles-without-Cripplegate. There has been a church here since Saxon times, situated outside the wall at Cripplegate.

The present building is late 14th-century perpendicular with a 17th-century tower. Buried here are John Foxe, author of the *Book of Martyrs*, Elizabethan sea dog Martin Frobisher, who fought against the Armada, map maker John Speed, and John Milton, author of *Paradise Lost*. Oliver Cromwell married Elizabeth Bourchier here in 1620.

☞ Across the water to the north of the church is the . . .

BARBICAN ARTS CENTRE
Open daily • Free

The largest arts and conference centre in Europe, home of the London Symphony Orchestra and London home of the Royal Shakespeare Company. The centre is spread over ten levels with a fabulous glass conservatory on the top floor and a huge art gallery on two lower floors where there is a constant mix of exhibitions on art and culture, fashion, architecture, design and photography.

☞ Exit the Arts Centre through the main north door and turn left on to Beech Street for Barbican station.

CHAPTER SIX

The Jubilee Line

Dollis Hill comes nearer to being a paradise than any other home I ever occupied

Mark Twain

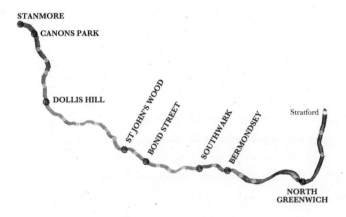

COLOUR: SILVER

YEAR OPENED: 1979

LENGTH: 22.5 MILES

FASCINATING FACT:

THE ONLY LINE ON THE TUBE NETWORK THAT
CONNECTS WITH ALL THE OTHER LINES

North and west from Baker Street

WALK ONE

ST JOHN'S WOOD

The only station on the Tube network whose name does not contain any of the letters in the word 'mackerel'. From here you can walk to the most famous recording studios in the world and the world's oldest sporting museum

ABBEY ROAD
Open 24 hours • Free

DIRECTIONS
Exit station and using the lights to your right cross over the main road into Grove End Road. Continue for quarter of a mile until you see a monument in the middle of the road at a junction. This is a memorial to the sculptor Edward Onslow Ford (1852–1901) who lived nearby. Turn right and the crossing is in front of you.

Here is possibly the most famous pedestrian crossing in the world. You can tell from the traffic jam caused by fans from all over the world posing on the crossing as they attempt to recreate the iconic cover of the Beatles' 1969 *Abbey Road* album. As a quiz master this place is close to my heart since it provides one of my favourite quiz questions – 'In what order are the Beatles crossing the road on the Abbey Road album cover?' Few people get it right first time. The yellow VW Beetle featured on the cover belonged to someone living in an apartment across the road and is now a prize exhibit at the Volkswagen museum in Wolfsburg.

☞ Cross the road using the pedestrian crossing, turn right and almost immediately on your left are . . .

ABBEY ROAD STUDIOS

You can't miss the studios because the road-side wall in front of them is always covered in Beatle-related graffiti, although the council do paint it over every three months. The most famous recording studios in the world, home to the world's largest purpose-built recording studio (Studio One), are hidden away in a modest 19th-century villa set back from the road, and it is spine-tingling to think that some of best-loved and most renowned music ever written, be it classical, pop or film soundtrack, was recorded right here.

No. 3 Abbey Road was bought by The Gramophone Company, which became EMI, in 1929 and they converted it into the world's first custom-built studio complex. It opened in 1931 with a performance by the London Symphony Orchestra of Sir Edward Elgar's *Pomp and Circumstance* conducted by the composer himself. A green plaque on the wall of the house commemorates the event. The following year Elgar conducted 15-year-old Yehudi Menuhin performing Elgar's *Violin Concerto*. In 1958 the studios ventured into rock music when Cliff Richard recorded his first single there, 'Move It', regarded as the first European rock and roll single. In 1962 the Beatles, produced by George Martin, recorded their first single at the studios, 'Love Me Do' – they would go on to record 90 per cent of their songs there before they split in 1970. During their time there the Beatles pioneered a number of recording techniques on their albums, including flanging and multi-track recording. In 1967 they made history when they performed 'All You Need is Love' before an audience of 350 million for the first ever world-wide satellite television link up. They called their penultimate album *Abbey Road* after the road, not the studio, which was then called EMI Studios. The studios changed their name to Abbey Road Studios in honour of the album . . .

Unfortunately, most of the time all you can do is gaze at the studios from the road and imagine what is going on inside, although there is the occasional open day.

LORD'S CRICKET GROUND
Open daily for tours • Charge

DIRECTIONS
As for Abbey Road but when you reach the memorial to Edward Onslow Ford, turn left instead of right and proceed down Grove End Road to the traffic lights.
Turn left and on your left is the Grace Gate.

The home of cricket and the MCC, Lord's is named after the Yorkshire wine trader and cricketer Thomas Lord, who came to London in the 1780s to restore his family's fortune, which had been sequestered after his father supported the '45 Jacobite Rising. Lord got work as a groundsman at an amateur cricket club in Islington called the White Conduit Club and soon proved himself a useful bowler. In 1787 the club members approached Lord to find them a new ground closer to London and so he prepared a pitch for them in Dorset Fields in Marylebone (now Dorset Square). The club changed its name to Marylebone Cricket Club and in 1788 laid down a new Code of Laws for cricket, which were soon adopted throughout the game – the MCC is to this day the authority on the laws of cricket. The first match played at 'Lord's Cricket Ground' was between Middlesex and Essex in 1787. In 1811 Dorset Fields was becoming built up so Lord's moved north to a new ground in St John's Wood. Not long afterwards Lord found out that the new Regent's Canal was to be built through the ground and so pocketed a tidy sum in compensation money and moved up the road to the present location. The first match was played at this Lord's Cricket Ground in 1814. And at each of the three Lord's Cricket Grounds the spectators entered via Thomas Lord's wine shop. He was eventually bought out and retired a wealthy man.

MCC MUSEUM
Open daily • Charge

The MCC Museum, which can be visited Separately from the tour, opened in 1953 and is the oldest sporting museum in the world. It covers the history of cricket and the MCC from the early 18th century to the present day, with material on the great players and events. Highlights include cricket's most precious jewel, the original

Ashes urn, the stuffed sparrow bowled out by Jahangir Kahn in 1936, cricket gear belonging to great players, such as Jack Hobbs and Don Bradman, and memorabilia associated with cricket's most famous player, W.G. Grace.

WALK TWO

DOLLIS HILL

A short walk around Dollis Hill, taking in a Prime Ministerial safe house, the birthplace of computers and a wartime bunker

American author Mark Twain famously referred to Dollis Hill as a paradise after staying at Dollis Hill House in the summer of 1900. The house is no longer there, alas – it was demolished in 2012 – but the grounds form one of London's least known yet most attractive green spaces, Gladstone Park.

☞ Take the north exit from the station, turn right and immediately left into Hamilton Road. Go to the end, turn left and take the bridge over the railway into Gladstone Park. Climb the hill to enjoy the spectacular views over London and explore the site of . . .

Dollis Hill House. Built in 1823 by Joseph Finch, the small Regency house that stood here inspired the poet Felicia Hemans in 1827 to write the lines made famous by Noël Coward, 'The stately homes of England, how beautiful they stand!' The house subsequently passed into the hands of Liberal peer and dog breeder Lord Tweedmouth, creator of the golden retriever, and then became the home of his daughter and her husband

Lord Aberdeen. They were good friends with four times Prime Minister William Gladstone, who would often come to stay, commenting that he felt better at Dollis Hill than anywhere else. He found Dollis Hill a wonderful retreat from the stresses of his political life and particularly loved to take a dip in the pond in front of the house, which is still there, now inhabited by ducks.

In 1900 Mark Twain came to stay as a guest of newspaper owner Hugh Gilzean-Reid and wrote, 'I have never seen any place that was so satisfactorily situated, with its noble trees and stretch of country, and everything that went to make life delightful, and all within a biscuit's throw of the metropolis of the world.' In 1901 the house was purchased by the local authority, who made the grounds into a park, which was named in honour of Dollis Hill's most celebrated visitor, William Gladstone. There is also a commemorative brass to the Grand Old Man in the lovely medieval church of St Mary's in Willesden at the bottom of the hill, where Gladstone would read the lesson on a Sunday when staying at Dollis Hill.

During the First World War the house was used as a hospital and in 1941 Winston Churchill's War Cabinet met there. The house was then turned into a restaurant, but it slowly fell into disrepair and, following two arson attacks, was finally demolished in 2012. The walled garden is beautifully maintained as a rose garden and the stables are run as a workshop, art gallery and exhibition space showing works by local artists and emerging artists from around Britain. There is also a tea shop.

The imposing building on top of the hill north of Gladstone Park is now luxury apartments, but was originally the Post Office Research Centre, opened in 1933 by Prime Minister

Ramsay MacDonald. In 1943 a team of engineers led by Tommy Flowers built the world's first programmable electronic computer there. Called Colossus, it was used at Bletchley Park to decipher German codes. A road at the back of the building is called Flowers Close in honour of Tommy Flowers.

PADDOCK

15 minutes ● Occasional pre-booked tours ● Charge

By Brook Road, at the north-west corner of the Post Office Research Centre site, now occupied by a housing estate, there is a low windowless structure made of modern brick with steps leading down to a grey steel door. This is the entrance to Paddock, an underground bunker that was constructed at the beginning of the Second World War as a safe alternative Cabinet War Room. Winston Churchill visited several times but the War Cabinet met there only once, in October 1940. Churchill found the bunker and its facilities uncomfortable and when they next gathered there in 1941 he took the War Cabinet down the hill to Dollis Hill House for their meeting instead.

Paddock is occasionally open for tours run by Subterranea Britannica whose website is www.subbrit.org.uk/sb-sites/sites/p/paddock/index.shtml

WALK THREE

CANONS PARK

A baroque masterpiece in Metroland

A short walk will bring you to one of the most extraordinary buildings in London, the only parish church in Britain built in the Continental Baroque style.

ST LAWRENCE CHURCH, LITTLE STANMORE

Open Sundays or by appointment • Free

DIRECTIONS
Exit station and turn left into Whitchurch Lane.
You will find the church on your left.

While pleasant enough, the exterior of this small church set in a quiet north London suburban street in no way prepares you for the glories within. The tower is early 16th-century but the rest of the church was rebuilt in 1717 in Continental Baroque style for James Brydges, 1st Duke of Chandos. Brydges had made a fortune as paymaster-general of the forces abroad during the War of Spanish Succession and was busy spending his riches on filling Cannons, his palatial new house at the other end of Canons Park, with expensive artworks and furniture. The church was to be his burial place and was thus decked out in suitable splendour, with the walls and ceilings covered in paintings, the ceiling by Louis Laguerre and other work by Antonio Bellucci. There are box pews, elaborate ironwork and beautifully carved woodwork, much of it by Grinling Gibbons, including the magnificent organ case, which houses an instrument played by George Frideric Handel, the Duke's composer-in-residence.

Added to the north side of the church in 1735, and today viewed through wrought-iron gates, is the Chandos Mausoleum, where the Duke lies beneath a vast monument showing him dressed in Roman garb, sporting a Georgian wig and flanked by the kneeling figures of his two wives, Mary and Cassandra, who rest here with him. The mausoleum was designed by James Gibbs in 1717 and the monument by Grinling Gibbons. The classical *trompe-l'oeil* paintings on the walls and the ceiling, which is a miniature copy of the dome of the Pantheon in Rome, are by Gaetano Brunetti.

The church is open for viewing during the summer on Sundays from 2–5pm or 2–4pm and, during the winter on Sundays from 2–4pm, but can be visited at other times by calling 020 8952 0019 in advance.

Once you have sampled the delights of the church, Canons Park itself is a very pretty place to stroll around. The Duke of Chandos lost his fortune in the South Sea Bubble of 1720 and his great house Cannons was pulled down in 1747, replaced by the Georgian house that stands there now at the north end of the park, and is occupied by a school. The contents of Cannons were dispersed around the country and some items can still be seen in London. There is a statue of George II in Golden Square, a panel carved by Grinling Gibbons in the Victoria & Albert Museum and a number of paintings in the National Gallery – and it is thought that the Ionic columns at the front of the National Gallery came from the grand Cannons colonnade.

WALK FOUR

STANMORE

An iconic piece of Britain's wartime heritage

BENTLEY PRIORY
30 minutes • Open Mon, Wed, Fri, Sat • Charge

DIRECTIONS
Turn left out of the station into London Road, which, at the traffic lights after 500 yards (450 m), becomes The Broadway. Continue to the next major traffic

lights and bear left into Church Road. After 500 yards
(450 m), having passed the church on your left, turn right
into Old Lodge Way and this will lead you into
Bentley Priory Park and Nature Reserve. Follow the
main path through the park (signposted) until you
reach the main gates to the Priory, a pleasant
10–15 minute walk.

Bentley Priory was built in 1775 on the site of an Augustinian
priory and extended in 1788 by Sir John Soane for the 1st
Marquess of Abercorn. It later became the last home of Queen
Adelaide, widow of William IV, and is where she died. After
serving as a hotel and a girls' school, the Priory was taken over
by the RAF and during the Second World War was the headquarters of RAF Fighter Command under Air Chief Marshal
Sir Hugh Dowding. In 2011 the house and immediate grounds
were bought by a property developer but the major part of
the priory was retained as the Bentley Priory Battle of Britain
Museum.

The museum, of which the building itself is the star attraction, tells the story of Bentley Priory, with particular focus on
its role as Fighter Command HQ during the Battle of Britain.
Dowding's office is preserved with its original furnishings while
the main museum gallery, where artefacts, trophies, uniforms,
photographs and other memorabilia are on display, is situated
in the old Officers' Mess.

This is a slightly longer walk, about 1½ miles (2.4 km)
(30 minutes), but much of it is through parkland, and the
museum, plus the stunning views over London once you get
there, make it well worth the effort. There is also a bus, No. 142,

that stops right outside Stanmore station every 10–15 minutes and goes to Bentley Priory.

South and east from Baker Street

The eastern extension of the Jubilee line is the only section of the underground that has glass safety screens across the platforms to prevent people from falling on to the track.

WALK FIVE

BOND STREET
Also served by Central Line

WALLACE COLLECTION
Open daily • Free

DIRECTIONS
From the station walk west along Oxford Street and then turn right up Duke Street. Manchester Square is at the end with Hertford House on the far side (north).

The Wallace Collection was gathered together between 1760 and 1880, the work of the first four Marquesses of Hertford and the 4th Marquess's illegitimate son Sir Richard Wallace. The latter's widow left the collection to the nation on the condition that every item remained in London and that no object was ever sold or loaned out. Hertford House in Manchester Square, where the collection is housed, was built in the 1780s for the

4th Duke of Manchester so that he could take advantage of the good duck shooting nearby. After serving as the Spanish embassy it was acquired by the 2nd Marquess of Hertford as his London townhouse, was then let out by the 3rd Marquess to the French embassy, and used by the 4th Marquess, who lived in Paris, to house his growing art collection. His son Richard Wallace moved from Paris to London in 1871, bringing the Paris collection with him, and redeveloped Hertford House, creating a range of galleries in which to display the works of art. After his death the house opened as a public museum in 1900 and has been open seven days a week ever since, except during the two world wars.

The collection is displayed over 28 rooms and contains over 5,000 objects. It is particularly noted for its collection of 18th-century French artworks, the best outside France, and is rich in paintings, furniture and Sèvres porcelain, some of it having once belonged to Marie Antoinette. Much of it was collected by the 4th Marquess at a time when, following the French Revolution, such artworks were of little interest to the French and could be purchased relatively inexpensively. There is also a fine armoury, a set of Limoges enamels, sculptures and some rare Italian pottery. Amongst the paintings are Frans Hals's *The Laughing Cavalier*, Jean-Honoré Fragonard's *The Swing*, Thomas Gainsborough's *Mrs Mary Robinson*, Rubens's *Landscape with a Rainbow*, Rembrandt's *The Artist's Son* and *Lady with a Fan* by Velazquez. The Wallace Collection is almost too heady for a single visit, but because it is permanent and always open, this is somewhere you can dip into and nourish the soul at any time.

WALK SIX

SOUTHWARK

A Victorian masterpiece

KIRKALDY TESTING MUSEUM
Open first Sunday of every month • Charge

DIRECTIONS
Exit station and cross Blackfriars Road towards the
tall glass building at traffic lights to your left. Turn left
and walk under the railway bridge down Blackfriars
Road, past Prince William Henry pub and then
next right into Burrell Street. Go under the railway to
the end, left and right into Southwark Street. The
museum is 100 yards (90 m) on your right.

This is home of the Universal Testing Machine, designed by
Scottish engineer David Kirkaldy, built in 1865, and installed
here in its own purpose-built testing house in 1874. The
hydraulically operated machine was used to test the strength
of materials such as iron and steel, and of structures large and
small made from such materials from all over the world. In 1867
the machine was employed to test parts of the Eads Bridge over
the Mississippi at St Louis, the longest arch bridge in the world
when it was built. Then it was employed to examine samples of
the failed railway bridge over the River Tay in Scotland, which
collapsed in a high wind in 1879 while a train was crossing,
causing the loss of 70 lives. It was also used to test parts for
the Skylon tower erected on the South Bank for the Festival of
Britain in 1951 and to analyse material from the Comet airliner

that crashed off Elba in 1954. The Comet was the world's first passenger jet airliner but suffered a number of catastrophic crashes in 1953–4, and Kirkcaldy's testing machine was instrumental in tracing the cause to metal fatigue.

Visitors are taken on a tour of the workshop where a variety of different testing machines are displayed and demonstrated, and can try out a testing machine for themselves. The highlight of the tour is a demonstration of Kirkaldy's original Universal Testing Machine itself.

WALK SEVEN

BERMONDSEY

A short walk through Bermondsey and Rotherhithe to Rotherhithe Overground station, taking in a view that inspired Turner, a royal retreat, a smugglers' pub, a famous church, a pub made from the timbers of the Mayflower, a unique film library, a museum dedicated to Britain's greatest engineer and the world's first underwater tunnel . . .

☞ Exit station and cross over the main road at pedestrian lights. Turn right and then left into Wilson Grove, named after a Rotherhithe man, Captain Henry Wilson of the East India Company. Go to the end and turn right on Bermondsey Wall East. Walk along the river until you see some cherry trees on your left and a sign saying . . .

Cherry Gardens. All that remains of a 17th-century pleasure garden of that name where Samuel Pepys would come to buy cherries for his wife. Stop here and take in the spectacular view of Tower Bridge and the City. In front of you is Cherry Garden Pier – boats would sound their horns here if they wanted Tower Bridge to open for them. In J.M.W. Turner's famous picture *The Fighting Temeraire*, painted in 1839, the old battle-ship, a veteran of Trafalgar, is seen from the Cherry Gardens being towed by a steamer to the breaker's yard, the sun setting behind her to signify the end of the era of sail. Turner was using a certain amount of artistic licence here, with his sunset appearing in the east rather than the west. The picture now hangs in the National Gallery.

☞ Continue along the riverside until you come to a large expanse of lawn on your right dotted with some scant ruins. This is the site of . . .

Edward III's Moated Manor. Built in 1353 on a small island beside the Thames when this was marshland, the royal manor house here consisted of a large stone house built around a central courtyard. It was surrounded by a moat on three sides and open to the river on the north side so that at high tide the king could arrive by boat and go straight into the house via the steps leading up through the gatehouse. It is thought that the house was used for the king to practise his falconry.

The Angel. Right next to the royal manor house, and with a balcony extending out over the Thames, the Angel sits on the site of an inn called the Salutation established by the monks of Bermondsey Abbey in the 15th century. By the 17th century it had been renamed The Angel and is referred to in Pepys's diary as 'the famous Angel'. Judge Jeffreys would come here to sit on the balcony and watch the hangings at Execution Dock across the river. Captain Cook prepared for his voyages of exploration here; Turner and Whistler painted the Thames from here.

☞ Walk on through King's Stairs Gardens, bear right to pick up the footpath and you will find yourself at the start of London's longest street, Rotherhithe Street, which runs from here for 1½ miles (2.4 km) around the Rotherhithe peninsula. Head for the spire of . . .

St Mary's Church. Paid for by the parishioners themselves, mainly seamen and dockworkers, this beautiful church was built in 1715 on the site of a 13th-century building undermined by flooding. It possesses one of England's most precious musical masterpieces, an 18th-century organ made by the renowned organ maker John Byfield and installed in 1764. It is celebrated far and wide for its glorious tones and attracts eminent organists from all over the world to play it. Another treasured possession is the Bishop's Chair, which is made from timbers salvaged from HMS *Temeraire*, subject of Turner's evocative painting (*see* above).

St Mary's has always been associated with mariners and buried in the churchyard is Christopher Jones, Captain of the *Mayflower*, which was crewed by Rotherhithe men and sailed from Rotherhithe at the start of the voyage that took the Pilgrim Fathers to the New World in 1620. Jones was buried somewhere in the churchyard in 1622 at the age of 55. The *Mayflower* is commemorated across the road from the church by . . .

The Mayflower pub. In 1620 the inn here was called the Shippe. The *Mayflower* was moored on the Thames nearby, before it set sail on its epic voyage to the New World. The following year the ship returned to its moorings here and was eventually allowed to rot, with some of the timbers being used to rebuild the Shippe, which by then was known as the Spread Eagle. In 1957 the inn was renamed the Mayflower in honour of its illustrious connection with that famous ship. To this day it is the only place in Britain licensed to sell US stamps, and you can still sup a beer while standing on the riverside balcony made out of the timbers that carried the Founding Fathers to America.

☞ Just over the road at 119 Rotherhithe Street is . . .

THE ROTHERHITHE PICTURE RESEARCH LIBRARY

Open Mon-Fri, 10am–4pm, weekends by appointment ● Free

Housed in an old granary built from reclaimed ships' timbers, the library opened in 1975 as a not for profit educational reference library where visitors can access volumes full of every kind of visual reference material, from postcards to magazine illustrations, from catalogue and book plates to original photographs, drawings and prints. The building is also the home of Sands Film Studios, which offers film production facilities, a free cinema club and a costume workshop.

☞ Continue along Rotherhithe Street and you will see on your right the . . .

BRUNEL MUSEUM
Open daily • Charge

Celebrating the life and works of Britain's greatest engineer, Isambard Kingdom Brunel, the museum is located in the engine house that once housed the steam pumps used to extract water from the world's first underwater tunnel, the Thames Tunnel, which runs along underneath. The tunnel was constructed by Brunel and his father Marc Brunel between 1825 and 1843, using a new tunnelling shield technique inspired by watching a worm nibbling its way through a piece of wood and passing the material along its body to be ejected at the back. The Thames Tunnel marked the beginning of the London underground and was the prototype for tunnels everywhere. Originally designed to take horse-drawn carriages, for 20 years it was only ever used by pedestrians and soon became a major tourist attraction visited by two million people every year. In 1865 the tunnel was bought by the East London Railway Company and converted for use by trains and is still today a part of the Tube system. The shaft and grand entrance hall by which visitors accessed the tunnel, and which was also used for acrobatic and tight-rope walking shows, was closed off. In 2015, after being abandoned for 150 years, the space was opened up again and visitors to the Brunel Museum can now descend into the hall and experience this historic chamber once more. It is a breathtaking adventure. On special occasions there are walks through the tunnel itself.

☞ On exiting the museum, follow signs to Rotherhithe station. The unusual horseshoe-shaped shafts of the Thames Tunnel can be clearly seen from the station platforms. Those wishing to pass through the tunnel should take the train north to Wapping, or if you wish to return to the Jubilee line then take the train south to Canada Water and change.

WALK EIGHT

NORTH GREENWICH

Built to handle large numbers of visitors to the Millennium Dome, North Greenwich is one of the biggest stations on the underground. From here you can visit the world's biggest dome, a flight simulator and London's only cable-car ride

THE O2 OR MILLENNIUM DOME
Open daily • Charge

Built amidst much controversy to celebrate the start of the third millennium, the Dome stands on the edge of the Greenwich Prime Meridian. With a diameter of 1,198 ft (365 m) it is the largest dome and the largest single-roofed structure in the world and has been the scene of some memorable moments – here on 1 January 2000 a bemused Queen Elizabeth II held hands with Tony Blair while singing 'Auld Lang Syne', and James Bond fell onto the roof from an exploding hot-air balloon during the opening credits of the 1999 film *The World Is Not Enough*. The Dome is now a successful music and entertainment venue, the O2, which includes a concert arena, cinema, exhibition area, bowling, night clubs and restaurants. It is now possible to climb up the Dome's roof, attached to a safety harness and with a guide, and experience exhilarating views of East London from an observation platform at the top. Booking required.

EMIRATES AVIATION EXPERIENCE
Open daily • Charge

Located next to the cable-car entrance, this exhibition uses state-of-the-art technology, interactive displays, films and visual aids to tell the story of commercial air travel. There are life-size models of modern aircraft, a virtual wind tunnel and you can try your hand at flying a Boeing 777 or Airbus A380 on the world's first public commercial flight simulators.

EMIRATES AIR LINE
Open daily • Charge

The first and only cable-car over the Thames opened in 2012. Just over half a mile (0.8 km) long, it links the Greenwich Peninsula to the Royal Docks and carries passengers across the river at a height of almost 300 feet (90 m). The views are sensational and in blowy conditions the journey can be quite bracing as the gondola sways from side to side in the wind. You can either make a single journey and pick up the DLR from Royal Victoria or make a return journey back to North Greenwich station. The ride is on the Oyster Card system.

CHAPTER SEVEN

The Metropolitan Line

O, as I trace again thy winding hill,
Mine eyes admire, my heart adores thee still,
Thou drooping elm! beneath whose boughs I lay,
And frequent mused the twilight hours away

'Lines Written beneath an Elm in the Churchyard of Harrow'
Lord Byron

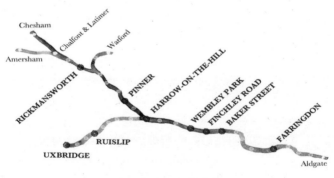

COLOUR: MAGENTA

YEAR OPENED: 1863

LENGTH: 42 MILES

FASCINATING FACT:

THE WORLD'S FIRST UNDERGROUND RAILWAY
(PADDINGTON TO FARRINGDON STREET)

North-west from Baker Street

WALK ONE

BAKER STREET
Also served by Circle, Hammersmith & City,
Bakerloo and Jubilee Lines

One of the original stations on the Metropolitan Line, the world's oldest underground railway, Baker Street is considered London Underground's flagship station. It is also the home of the TFL (Transport For London) Lost Property Office. Baker Street has ten platforms, more than any other underground station.

The name of Baker Street is known across the world through Gerry Rafferty's song 'Baker Street', with its glorious saxophone solo, and as the home of the world's most famous detective, Sherlock Holmes.

THE SHERLOCK HOLMES MUSEUM
Open daily • Charge

DIRECTIONS
Take Baker Street exit and turn right. Museum is
150 yards (137 m) along on the other side of the road.

The Sherlock Holmes Museum occupies a Georgian terraced house at the north end of Baker Street, and is identified by a blue plaque at first-floor level. It was a former boarding house of the kind where, according to the books, Holmes and Watson lived as tenants of Mrs Hudson. The real address is 239 Baker Street, but the house bears the number 221B by special permission of Westminster Council. According to local records of the 1890s a maid who worked in the boarding house went by the name of Holmes and a real-life Dr Watson, a manufacturer of artificial teeth, lived next door.

The interior of the house has been meticulously kitted out as described in the books. On the first floor is Holmes's bedroom and study, complete with fireside armchair (in which you can sit), deerstalker, magnifying glass, pipe, violin and Persian slippers. On the second floor are Mrs Hudson's room, at the front, and Dr Watson's room at the rear with his diary and handwritten notes on display. The rooms on the third floor contain an arrangement of wax models recreating scenes from the novels.

There is a small shop on the ground floor and visitors are welcomed into the house by Mrs Hudson. Mail sent to Sherlock Holmes from all over the world is delivered here.

A SHORT WALK AROUND MARYLEBONE

☞ Take Marylebone Road exit, turn left and follow signs to . . .

MADAME TUSSAUDS
Open daily • Charge

The most famous waxworks museum in the world has its roots in the Paris of the 1770s. Madame Tussaud was born in France in 1761 and was taught the art of modelling in wax by the Swiss physician Dr Philippe Curtius, for whom her mother worked. Her very first waxwork was of Voltaire, while other early models included Jean-Jacques Rousseau and Benjamin Franklin. During the French Revolution she was employed making death masks of some of the victims of the Terror.

When Dr Curtius died, Madame Tussaud inherited his collection of waxworks and created a travelling exhibition, which she took around Europe, ending up in Britain in 1802. Unable to return to France because of the Napoleonic Wars, she took her show round Britain and Ireland to great acclaim and established a permanent base in Baker Street in 1835. Madame Tussaud died in 1850 and the exhibition was taken over by her son. It was moved to its home premises in Marylebone Road in 1884.

Before photography, waxwork models were the only means by which most people could see what the famous people of the day looked like and Madame Tussauds was, in some ways, the *Hello!* magazine of its time. Today the museum provides commentary on the transient world of celebrity, displaying a constantly changing selection of the top celebrities of the day alongside more enduring historic figures, royalty, world leaders, film stars, musicians and artists. A highlight is the world's first animatronic, a waxwork of a sleeping Madame du Barry, mistress to Louis XV, whose bosom rises and falls as she breathes. It is the oldest item on display in the museum and was made by Dr Curtius in 1763.

The ever popular Chamber of Horrors shows the original bloody death masks made by Madame Tussaud, including those of Marie Antoinette, Robespierre and Louis XVI, as well as notorious villains and serial killers, such as Vlad the Impaler, upon whom Dracula was based, Genghis Khan, Guy Fawkes, Dr Crippen, Stalin and Adolf Hitler. There is also a dimly lit haunted dungeon where live actors pose amongst the waxworks and then spring to life, causing some visitors to run screaming from the chamber.

☞ Exit museum and continue east along Marylebone Road for 200 yards (180 m) until you reach York Gate on the left. The music museum is on the corner.

ROYAL ACADEMY OF MUSIC MUSEUM
Open Mon-Sat • Free

Housed in a beautiful John Nash villa on the corner of York Gate and Marylebone Road, the Museum of the Royal Academy of Music, Britain's oldest conservatoire, houses a fascinating collection of musical instruments, manuscripts and scores, artwork and materials. There are three permanent galleries, the Piano Gallery, the String Gallery and the Ground Floor Gallery, the last of which contains the History of the Academy display and hosts temporary exhibitions and displays.

Highlights of the museum include a Stradivarius violin made in 1709 and played for Marie Antoinette, one of Sir Henry Wood's conducting batons, letters of Felix Mendelssohn, and Gilbert and Sullivan's original score for *The Mikado*.

On most days members of staff can be heard playing some of the museum's historic instruments and there are frequent lectures and musical events.

☞ Now cross Marylebone Road to . . .

ST MARYLEBONE CHURCH
11 minutes • Open daily • Free

Neo-classical style church built in 1817 by Thomas Hardwick to replace an older church that stood just to the south in Marylebone High Street. The north front of the present church on Marylebone Road is a Corinthian portico based on the Parthenon in Rome, while the domed steeple above it is crowned with a miniature temple surrounded by angel caryatids. They were clothed in gold leaf at the expense of former churchwarden and surgeon Sir Henry Souttar, who in 1925 became the first surgeon ever to operate on the human heart.

Author Wilkie Collins (*The Woman in White*) was baptised here in 1824. Charles Dickens, who lived nearby (*see* below), had a number of his children baptised in the church and made St Marylebone the setting for the christening of Paul Dombey in his novel *Dombey and Son*. In September 1846 poet Elizabeth Barrett stole out of her father's home in Wimpole Street and married Robert Browning in the church. A week later she left London, never to return, although it is said that whenever possible Robert returned on their wedding anniversary and kissed the church steps.

The crypt houses a Healing and Counselling Centre and occasional art exhibitions.

☞ Exit the church, turn right and right again, go through the cobbled churchyard and turn right onto Marylebone High Street where you will find . . .

THE OLD CHURCH GARDEN
Marylebone High Street • 13 minutes • Open daily • Free

An obelisk here marks the tomb of hymn writer and Methodist founder Charles Wesley. The garden is the site of the previous St Marylebone church, built originally in 1400, rebuilt in 1741 and demolished in 1949. A plaque tells us that amongst other notables buried here are James Gibbs, architect of St Martin-in-the-Fields, sculptor John Michael Rysbrack and painter George Stubbs. In 1773 playwright Richard Brinsley Sheridan was married to Elizabeth Ann Linley in the church here; Lord Byron was baptised here in 1788; Sir William Hamilton married Emma Hart here in 1791, and Emma's child by Lord Nelson, Horatia Nelson, was baptised here in 1803.

The earlier church was built in 1400 to replace the village church of Tybourne (Tyburn), which stood further south near the present-day Marble Arch. The church built here was called St Mary-by-the-Bourne (the Tybourne), and this became shortened to St Marylebone and so gave the district its name. The Elizabethan philosopher Francis Bacon was married to Alice Barnham in this earlier church in 1606, while the interior was portrayed by William Hogarth in the marriage scene from

The Rake's Progress (1735), which can be seen in the Sir John Soane Museum (*see* Holborn, Central line).

Just to the south on Marylebone High Street is one of London's premier bookshops, the original Daunt Books, housed in a former Edwardian bookshop. It was built in 1912 and is lined with beautiful oak galleries – the first custom-built bookshop in the world.

☞ Now retrace your steps to Baker Street station.

WALK TWO

FARRINGDON

Also served by Circle and Hammersmith & City Lines

Opened in 1863 as the eastern terminus of the Metropolitan Railway, the world's first underground railway. The only station to be on both the north/south Thameslink and east/west Crossrail (from 2018).

A SHORT CIRCULAR WALK FROM FARRINGDON STATION

☞ Exit station and turn right. Go straight across Farringdon Road into Greville Street, over Saffron Hill (home of Fagin in *Oliver Twist*) and turn left into the alleyway at the Bleeding Heart Tavern for . . .

Bleeding Heart Yard. Legend has it that the name commemorates the murder in 1626 of the beautiful Lady Elizabeth Hatton. During a ball at Hatton House, she danced with a smartly dressed gentleman ambassador who turned out to be the Devil in disguise. Next morning her body was found in the yard torn limb from limb but with her heart still beating and bleeding over the cobbles. Charles Dickens features Bleeding Heart Yard as the home of the Plornish family in *Little Dorrit*.

☞ A small gateway at the far side of the yard leads into . . .

Ely Place. From the end of the 13th century until 1772, when these terraced houses were built, this was the site of the Bishop of Ely's London home, during which time it wasn't part of London but an enclave of Cambridgeshire. Now Crown property, guarded by a set of ornate iron gates and beadle's lodge, it is the last private road in the City of London. John of Gaunt lived in Ely House after his Savoy Palace was sacked during the Peasant's Revolt in 1381 until his death in 1399, and here Shakespeare has him give his 'This royal throne of Kings, this sceptre'd isle' speech from *Richard II*. Halfway down Ely Place is . . .

ST ETHELDREDA'S CHURCH
Open daily • Free

Built in 1293 as the private chapel of the Bishops of Ely, this is the oldest Catholic church in England. It has an earlier crypt dating from 1251 and a beautiful west window from 1300. In 1373 a cloister was added and this is where Henry VIII first met his future Archbishop of Canterbury, Thomas Cranmer.

A narrow alleyway off the west side of Ely Place leads to the **Olde Mitre Tavern**, built by the Bishop of Ely in 1546 for his servants and extended in 1782. Inside there is the stump of a cherry tree around which Elizabeth I danced with her favourite, Sir Christopher Hatton. Having sampled the pub, continue down the passageway to emerge on . . .

Hatton Garden. The centre of Britain's diamond trade, this street is named after the above-mentioned Sir Christopher Hatton, who leased the land here from the Bishops of Ely in 1576. Chancellor to Elizabeth I, he was sponsor of Sir Francis Drake's voyage round the world in the *Golden Hind*, which was named for the golden hind on the Hatton family crest.

Turn right and walk north on Hatton Garden passing, on your right, a beautiful Wren-inspired building put up as a chapel after the Great Fire of London in 1666. It later became a charity school, hence the figures of children in 18th-century costume either side of the doorway. On the last building on the right, where Hatton Garden meets Clerkenwell Road, a blue plaque informs us that here in 1884 Sir Hiram Maxim designed and manufactured the Maxim gun, the world's first recoil-operated machine-gun, capable of firing 600 rounds a minute. Directly across Clerkenwell Road is the huge double portico of . . .

St Peter's Italian Church, set beneath two mosaics showing the Miracle of the Fishes and Jesus giving the Keys of the Kingdom of Heaven to St Peter. Built in 1863 to serve Clerkenwell's growing Italian community, St Peter's was then the only Roman basilica style church in Britain. If you can gain entry, the interior is magnificent.

☞ Now turn right, or if you are leaving St Peter's turn left, and walk east on Clerkenwell Road. Take the left slip at the traffic lights, cross Farringdon Road and take the small road directly ahead leading uphill to . . .

Clerkenwell Green, now concreted over but blessed with a few trees and a whisper of old village atmosphere. In Victorian times the Green was a centre for radical and political gatherings, and in 1890 was the starting point for the world's first ever May Day march. A May Day march still leaves from here every year. The smart Georgian building on the left, with its appropriately red door, is the . . .

MARX MEMORIAL LIBRARY
Restricted opening • Free

This building was put up in 1738 to house the Welsh Charity School. In 1893, with funds donated by William Morris, it became the home of the Twentieth Century Press, publishers of *Justice*, the newspaper of the Social Democratic Federation, Britain's first organised Socialist party. Lenin worked here while exiled from Russia and from 1902 to 1903 edited and printed 17 editions of the underground journal *Iskra* here, which were then smuggled into Russia. In 1933, on the fiftieth anniversary of Karl Marx's death, the Marx Memorial Library was established here and now holds some 45,000 books, pamphlets, journals and newspapers on Marxism, Socialism and the history of the working classes. Highlights on display include 'The Printers' Collection', the archive of the British print unions, complete runs of the *Daily Worker* and *Morning*

Star newspapers, the world's largest collection of material on the Spanish Civil War, a red Hammersmith Socialist Society banner stitched personally by William Morris, and a rather magnificent fresco painted by Jack Hastings in 1935 showing a worker, flanked by Lenin, Marx and Engels, breaking free from his chains and destroying Big Ben. The library is open for the public to look around between 1pm and 2pm from Monday to Thursday. Admission free.

☞ Exit the library, turn left and cross the road to the . . .

Crown Tavern, where Lenin would often go for a drink. It was called the Crown & Anchor then, and it is said that right here is where Lenin met Stalin for the first time, in 1905.

☞ Exit the Crown and turn right to visit . . .

St James's Church, occupying a fine elevated situation above the green. Built in 1792, it's an agreeable building and unique as the only known church accredited to architect James Carr, a local man. The crypt, with its vaulted brick ceiling, is spectacular and there are some interesting monuments in the church itself, including that of Henry Penton after whom the area of Pentonville is named. Thomas Rolfe, the son of John Rolfe and Pocahontas, married Elizabeth Washington in the previous church that stood on this site, in 1632.

☞ Return to the green and turn left on to Aylesbury Street and after 100 yards (90 m) turn right at the Indian restaurant into . . .

Jerusalem Passage. A green plaque on the wall of the factory building on the corner informs us that here, in the early

18th century, stood the house of Thomas Britton the Musical Coalman. A coal merchant by day, Britton was something of an impresario by night, hosting musical evenings in a small room above his shop where ordinary folk could come along and hear some of the great musicians of the day. His star guest was Handel, who would play the harpsichord, and on more than one occasion treated the audience here to the first performance of a new composition.

☞ Walk along Jerusalem Passage and emerge into cobbled St John's Square.

This was the site of Clerkenwell Priory, the grounds of which stretched from here to Smithfield. The Priory was founded in the reign of Henry II as the English home of the Order of the Knights Hospitallers of St John of Jerusalem, which was set up in Jerusalem in 1023 to care for sick or destitute pilgrims to the Holy Land. The Order in England was dissolved by Henry VIII in 1540 but revived in the 19th century and is today most visible in the guise of St John's Ambulance.

On the left, on the site of the old priory church and now hidden behind a 1950s façade, is the much restored and rebuilt . . .

ST JOHN'S CHURCH
Open Mon-Sat • Free

The outline of the original round priory church, consecrated by the Patriarch of Jerusalem in 1185 and larger even than the Temple church, is marked out on the square. The whole area was badly bombed in the Second World War and the present church is a reconstruction of the wrecked 19th-century building, but the magnificent crypt of the original priory church survives beneath. Over 60 feet (18 m) long with five vaulted bays, this is one of the best examples of Norman work in London. The entrance is through the iron gate between the stone columns and there is also a small museum and Garden of Remembrance.

☞ Now cross Clerkenwell Road and in front of you is . . .

ST JOHN'S GATE
Open Mon-Sat • Free

Built in 1504, this was the priory's main gatehouse. It has since been put to many different uses including, in the 18th century, a coffee house run by Richard Hogarth, father of artist William Hogarth, a printworks for *The Gentleman's Magazine*, during which time Dr Johnson was provided with a room in which to write his articles, and a pub, the Old Jerusalem Tavern, patronised by writers and artists including Charles Dickens. Today it is once more owned by the Order of St John as their headquarters. It now houses the larger part of the Museum of the Order of St John, which traces the history of the Order right back to its foundation in Jerusalem nearly 1,000 years ago. There are frequent guided tours of the gatehouse, for which a donation is suggested.

☞ Continue south on St John's Lane, take the second right, Albion Place, go over Britton Street into Benjamin Street, left at the end and right for Farringdon station.

WALK THREE

FINCHLEY ROAD
Also served by Jubilee Line

FREUD MUSEUM
Open Wed-Sun • Charge

DIRECTIONS
Exit station and cross Finchley Road at the lights.
Turn right and after 100 yards (91 m) turn left up the
slope of Trinity Walk. At the top turn left into
Maresfield Gardens. The museum is 200 yards
(182 m) along on the right, at No. 20.

Psychoanalyst Sigmund Freud and his family moved into this Queen Anne style house after escaping to London from the annexation of Austria by the Nazis in 1938. He died the following year but the house stayed in the family until the death of his youngest daughter Anna in 1982. She left wishes that it should become a museum dedicated to her father's life and work. Sigmund Freud's study has been preserved as it was in his lifetime, chock-a-block with antiquities, figurines and books. You can see the desk where he would sit and write into the small hours and, most thrilling, the original analytic couch on which his patients would recline during consultations. The rest of the house is furnished with items the family brought with them from Vienna including some superb Biedermeier chests and tables. On the landing there is a portrait of Sigmund Freud by Salvador Dali. Visitors can also stroll in the garden, again laid out as in Sigmund Freud's time.

There is a small shop in the conservatory on the ground floor and there are rooms given over to frequent exhibitions of contemporary art.

WALK FOUR

WEMBLEY PARK

Also served by Jubilee Line

The world's first fully integrated entertainment and exhibition venue

Originally a country estate with grounds by Humphrey Repton, Wembley Park was bought in 1889 by Sir Edward

Watkin, Chairman of the Metropolitan Railway, with the idea of creating a leisure complex for Londoners. It opened in 1894 with sports pitches, a boating lake, a music hall, its own railway station (Wembley Park) and what was intended to be the Great Tower of London, a 1,175 ft (358 m) high iron lattice tower, taller than the Eiffel Tower. The tower, known ever since as Watkin's Tower, was never completed and the stump was demolished in 1907.

In 1923 the famous 'twin towers' Empire Stadium opened for the FA Cup final of that year and became the centre-piece for the British Empire Exhibition of 1924–5. New amenities and transport facilities were built to cater for the exhibition, making Wembley Park the world's first fully integrated entertainment and exhibition venue.

SSE ARENA (WEMBLEY ARENA)
DIRECTIONS
Follow signs from the station

The first building you come to is the Empire Pool, built in 1934 for the second Empire Games, with a 60-metre swimming pool that included Europe's first wave machine and diving pool. Renamed Wembley Arena, the venue has been used for ice skating, boxing and horse shows and in 1950 staged its first music concerts. Known today as the SSE Arena, it is one of the world's top music venues and also hosts TV shows, such as *Britain's Got Talent*, *Dancing on Ice*, *Strictly Come Dancing* and the *X Factor* live shows. The original swimming pool, which was last used for the 1948 Olympic Games, is still preserved under the arena's floor.

WEMBLEY STADIUM
Open daily for tours • Charge

The New Wembley Stadium was opened in 2007 on the site of the 1923 Empire Stadium, where England won the World Cup in 1966 and where Live Aid was staged in 1985, in one of the largest ever global satellite live broadcasts. With a capacity of 90,000 the new Wembley is the largest stadium in the UK and the second largest in Europe behind Barcelona's Camp Nou. Home of England international football matches and the FA Cup final, the present stadium has a partially retractable roof supported by the landmark 440 ft (134 m) high Wembley Arch, which with a span of 1,033 ft (315 m) is the longest single-span roof structure in the world.

Square of Fame. Situated between Wembley Stadium and the SSE Arena is the Square of Fame, where artists appearing at the arena have left their handprints on bronze plaques embedded in the ground. Madonna was the first to have a plaque, in 2006. Others include Sir Cliff Richard, Kylie Minogue, Dolly Parton, Bryan Adams, Lionel Ritchie, Rick Parfitt and Francis Rossi of Status Quo, all four members of Westlife and Alice Cooper.

WALK FIVE

HARROW-ON-THE-HILL

Harrow-on-the-Hill sits 408 feet (124 m) above sea level and is one of London's least spoiled villages.

A WALK AROUND HARROW-ON-THE-HILL

☞ Take the south exit from the station and walk straight ahead to the main road. Cross over into the park and walk diagonally through the park towards the church spire at the top of the hill.

St Mary's Church. Charles II, staying at Windsor, was asked what he understood by the phrase 'the Church Visible' and in reply he pointed at the distant spire of St Mary's, still one of London's most prominent landmarks. It is 200 feet (61 m) tall and dates from 1450. The church was consecrated in 1094 but most of the present building is 15th-century.

> *Again I behold where for hours I have ponder'd,*
> *As reclining, at eve, on yon tombstone I lay;*
> *Or round the steep brow of the churchyard I wander'd,*
> *To catch the last gleam of the sun's setting ray.*
>
> Lord Byron

Byron was a pupil at Harrow School and would often come to the churchyard to ponder the superb views across London while seated on 'my favourite tomb, the Peachey Tomb'. He remembers such occasions in his poem 'Lines Written beneath an Elm in the Churchyard of Harrow'. The elm burned down long ago but the tomb is still there, south-west of the church, now caged in to protect it from souvenir hunters. The poem is reproduced on a memorial in front of it. Somewhere near the south porch is the unmarked grave of Allegra, Byron's illegitimate daughter by Claire Clairmont, stepsister of *Frankenstein* author Mary Shelley. Allegra, who was cruelly abandoned by her father and sent to a convent, died at the age of five and Byron had her embalmed body sent to Harrow asking for her to be buried under the elm tree, but this request was refused because of Byron's dissolute reputation. In 1980 a small memorial tablet to Allegra was placed near the spot.

Leave the churchyard via the lych-gate to the south and walk down between the buildings of the school.

On the wall of the building on your right, just past the oriel window, is a brass plaque recalling that, while standing on the school steps, Anthony Ashley-Cooper, later 7th Earl of Shaftesbury, saw a pauper's funeral pass by and felt so ashamed that he there and then dedicated his life to helping the poor.

Harrow School. The school was founded in 1572 by a wealthy local farmer John Lyon, who lies in the church. Seven British prime ministers were educated there, Spencer Perceval, Viscount Goderich, Robert Peel, Lord Aberdeen, Lord Palmerston, Stanley Baldwin and Sir Winston Churchill, as well as Pandit Nehru, first prime minister of India, King Hussein of Jordan, scriptwriter Richard Curtis, actor Benedict Cumberbatch and the American ornithologist after whom the world's most famous spy was named, James Bond.

On reaching the **High Street** continue into the village to enjoy the mix of Georgian and Victorian houses that line the street. Bear left at the fork and carry on the village green where there is a rare gantry sign of Henry VIII that recalls the King's Head Hotel, a fine Georgian building standing back on the west side of the green. This closed as a hostelry in the 1980s and was converted into apartments.

Retrace your steps to the school and carry on past the turning to the church, towards the chapel. Take the next left into Grove Hill, scene in 1899 of the first fatal accident involving a petrol motor car in Britain, as recorded on a notice set into the curve of the brick wall immediately on your right, beginning 'Take Heed'. A Daimler, being taken on a demonstration run by Mr E.R. Sewell, shed a wheel rim while going down Grove Hill and hit a kerb, pitching the driver and his passenger, 63-year-old Major James Richer, Department Head at the Army & Navy Stores, into the road. Sewell was killed on the spot, Major Richer died four days later.

Carry on down Grove Hill, taking heed, and after 100 yards (91 m) there is a plaque on a brick pillar on the left marking King Charles' Well, a spring where Charles I stopped to water his horses and look back at London while on the run from Cromwell's army in 1646.

Continue down Grove Hill, turn left at the bottom and return to the station.

Uxbridge Branch

WALK SIX

RUISLIP
Also served by Piccadilly Line

☞ Turn left outside the station approach and right at the lights into the modern high street. A short walk brings you to the heart of the old village of Ruislip, with a fine grouping of old buildings centred around the church.

St Martin's Church. A Norman church rebuilt in 1245 with a 15th-century tower. Of particular interest inside is a set of fine medieval wall paintings. Across the road from the church is . . .

MANOR FARM
Open Mon-Sat • Free

A heritage and culture centre has been built around the handsome 16th-century Manor Farm House. It sits on the site of an 11th-century Benedictine prior's house and is adjacent to the remains of a Norman motte and bailey castle. The Manor served as a manorial court and a working farmhouse until well into the 20th century. It now houses a small museum and interpretive centre. Nearby is . . .

The Great Barn. Dating from the 13th century, this is the oldest timber barn in Britain and the second largest after the barn in Harmondsworth near Heathrow. It is a wonderful space and is used for markets, functions, weddings, exhibitions and craft workshops.

The Little Barn. Built in the 16th century, this was converted into a library in 1937.

WALK SEVEN

UXBRIDGE
Also served by Piccadilly Line

THE BATTLE OF BRITAIN BUNKER
20 minutes • Open for tours on selected dates
(*see website*) • Free

DIRECTIONS
Take rear exit from station. Turn right then left at traffic lights into Montague Road. Follow to the end

and cross straight over main road at traffic lights into Honeycroft Hill. Take the fourth right onto Honey Hill, which becomes Vine Lane. Pass the entrance to ACS Hillingdon International School on your left, then take the next right onto St Andrew's Road. Follow St Andrew's Road to a large white house (Hillingdon House), then turn left. The entrance to the Battle of Britain Bunker is directly in front of you.

It was on leaving this bunker on 16 August 1940 that Prime Minister Winston Churchill uttered the immortal words, 'Never in the field of human conflict was so much owed by so many to so few.' Home of the Fighter Command No. 11 Group, the bunker came into commission in 1938, ten days before the outbreak of the Second World War. It housed the operations room from which the RAF fighter squadrons covering the south of England were controlled throughout the war, and in particular during the Battle of Britain in 1940. It was at the heart of the world's first integrated air defence system, which saved the country from the Luftwaffe air strikes intended to soften up Britain before Hitler's forces invaded.

The Bunker tour is based around the iconic flight operations room, set up as it would have been during the war, when aircraft movements were plotted by moving numbered blocks around on a large map table. There is also a museum with photographs, prints, uniforms and other RAF artefacts, and film footage shown in the old briefing room. The Bunker gives a unique insight into a particularly memorable part of Britain's wartime past. It is not an easy place to find but well worth the effort.

Amersham Branch

WALK EIGHT

PINNER

Pinner still retains its village atmosphere and is a pleasant place for a gentle stroll, with some delightful 16th-century half-timbered houses to see and a number of good local shops and pubs. Elton John was born here in 1947.

HEATH ROBINSON MUSEUM
Scheduled to open in May 2016 • Charge

DIRECTIONS
Exit the station, turn left, right at the end of Station Approach then next left under the railway bridge and left into Pinner Memorial Park. Follow the main concrete path to West House.

William Heath Robinson was an influential and popular cartoonist and illustrator whose wonderful drawings of dotty and unnecessarily complicated machines and inventions brought his name into the language. A 'Heath Robinson' contraption or something that is 'a bit Heath Robinson' is something crackpot, eccentric or impromptu, usually thrown together with whatever materials are at hand. Heath Robinson also illustrated books, including Charles Kingsley's *The Water Babies*, books by Hans Christian Andersen and Rudyard

Kipling, and many of the Professor Branestawm books. He lived at 75 Moss Lane from 1913 to 1918, and the museum in nearby West House is dedicated to the appreciation and preservation of his work, with permanent and temporary exhibition galleries showing his illustrations along with books, photographs, film and digital media that tell the story of his artistic career.

WALK NINE

RICKMANSWORTH

Penn and water

Rickmansworth is a pleasant small market town with a nice mix of old houses and shops. The narrow high street repays a gentle stroll.

THREE RIVERS MUSEUM
Mon-Fri afternoons, Sat 10am-4pm • Free

DIRECTIONS
Exit the station, turn right, and then right again underneath the railway, continue to the high street and turn left. The museum is on the left, just past the Church Street junction.

Basing House is the former home of William Penn, the founder of Pennsylvania, who lived there for five years following his marriage to Gulielma Springett in 1672. The building now houses the Three Rivers Museum, which tells the history of Rickmansworth and the surrounding area. The area is known as Three Rivers because it sits at the confluence of the rivers Gade, Colne and Chess. The museum contains a number of permanent and temporary displays highlighting Three Rivers as, amongst other things, an important junction on the Grand Union Canal and the former centre of Britain's paper-making industry.

BATCHWORTH CANAL CENTRE
Open daily • Charge for boat trips

DIRECTIONS
Exit the station, turn right, and then right again
underneath the railway. Continue to the high
street and turn left. After 200 yards (180m) turn
right down Church Street. Continue to the end,
curving past the church, and straight on at
the next junction. After 50 yards (45 m) the road
crosses the Grand Union Canal and on the left
is Batchworth Lock.

The headquarters of the Rickmansworth Waterways Trust is housed in an old stable block and pub. There is a shop, demonstrations of the lock in operation, a small display with books and maps about life on the canals, suggested canal walks, a café and trips along the canal in a historic narrow boat.

CHAPTER EIGHT

The Northern Line

I have conversed with the Spiritual Sun – I met him on Primrose Hill

William Blake

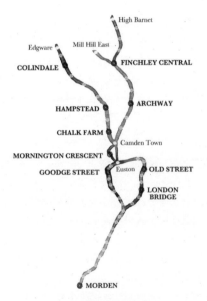

COLOUR: BLACK

YEAR OPENED: 1890 (BOROUGH TO STOCKWELL)

LENGTH: 36 MILES

FASCINATING FACT:

THE BOROUGH TO STOCKWELL SECTION OF THE NORTHERN LINE IS THE OLDEST DEEP LEVEL TUBE LINE

North from Camden Town – Edgware Branch

WALK ONE

CHALK FARM

PRIMROSE HILL

DIRECTIONS

To visit Primrose Hill, exit station, turn right, cross the
road at zebra crossing, turn right and left into Bridge
Approach. Go over the bridge and you are in Regent's
Park Road, the high street of Primrose Hill village.
Continue through the village to Primrose Hill itself
and climb the hill for spectacular views over London.

Primrose Hill village has long been one of London's most
sought-after addresses, home in the past to such luminaries as
Sylvia Plath, W.B. Yeats, philosopher Friedrich Engels, histo-
rian A.J.P. Taylor, authors Kingsley and Martin Amis and more
recently celebrity cook Jamie Oliver, fashion designer Stefano
Gabbana, *Fifty Shades of Grey* director Sam Taylor-Johnson,
high-street guru Mary Portas, model Suki Waterhouse, playwright Alan Bennett, comedian David Walliams, distinguished
journalist Sir Simon Jenkins and press baron's daughter
Elisabeth Murdoch. The village even once had its own 'set', the
Primrose Hill Set, young successful actors, models and musicians who lived in and around the area: Jude Law and Sadie

Frost, Ewan McGregor, Jonny Lee Miller, Sean Pertwee, Kate Moss, Noel Gallagher.

It is easy to see why Primrose Hill is so popular. Even though it isn't really a village at all, it has a charmingly bohemian, villagey feel, yet is close to the heart of London. Regent's Park Road is lined with attractive cafés, bistros, restaurants and individual shops full of character, such as the village greengrocer Yeoman's and Primrose Hill Books, one of London's favourite independent bookshops. Primrose Hill itself, 112 acres (45 ha) of wide, breezy lawn and trees rising to a superb viewpoint 206 feet (63 m) above sea level, really is named for the primroses that once grew here in abundance.

WALK TWO

HAMPSTEAD

'from a little village almost to a city'

Daniel Defoe

Hampstead is the deepest station on the Tube system 192 feet (59 m) below street level. The village of Hampstead is perhaps the most exclusive of London's relatively unspoiled villages and has more blue plaques than any other part of London. Once a thriving spa, then a haven for artists and left-wing intellectuals, the village is now the preserve of wealthy bankers and lawyers.

A WALK AROUND HAMPSTEAD

☞ Exit station and turn hard left down Hampstead High Street and immediately left into pedestrian alleyway Ginsberg Yard, which straight away becomes Flask Walk – where, in the 18th century, flasks of Hampstead well water could be obtained. It is lined with quirky shops (Keith Fawkes second-hand bookshop is famous) and the Flask pub. Carry on along Flask Walk, bear right at the green and then turn left into New End Square. (John Constable lived at 40 Well Walk, straight ahead, in 1827.)

BURGH HOUSE AND HAMPSTEAD MUSEUM
Open Wed, Thurs, Fri and Sun afternoons • Free

Burgh House was built during the reign of Queen Anne in 1704. In 1936 Rudyard Kipling came here to visit his daughter Elsie Bambridge, who lived in the house, on what turned out to be his last ever outing before he died. Today the house contains an art gallery and hosts exhibitions and concerts. Also here is Hampstead's local history museum, telling the story of Hampstead from prehistoric times to the present, with displays exploring Hampstead's days as an 18th-century spa to rival Bath and telling tales of the famous artists and writers who have lived in the village over the years. The lovely terraced garden was designed by Gertrude Jekyll.

☞ Exit the museum and turn right up New End Square to the White Bear pub. Turn right here and bear right along

Well Road. Go over Christchurch Hill and left up narrow Cannon Lane past the old parish lock-up, situated in the garden wall of Cannon Hall, once a magistrates' court. At the top turn left into Cannon Place past the gates of Cannon Hall where a blue plaque informs us that 'Sir Gerald du Maurier, Actor-Manager, lived here from 1916 until his death'. He was the father of novelist Daphne du Maurier and his nephews, the Llewelyn Boys, were the inspiration for the boys in *Peter Pan*. Continue along Cannon Place. Egyptologist Sir Flinders Petrie, whose collection can be found in the museum at UCL (*see* Euston Square, Hammersmith & City) lived at No. 5 on the right. Go past Christ Church and walk straight ahead across the pavement into Hampstead Square. Cross the main road in front of you, left and right into The Mount. Bear right at the top of the Mount and stop at the crossroads. Over to your right is the highest point in London, 440 feet (134 m) above sea level and site of the **Hampstead Observatory**, where on clear Friday, Saturday and Sunday evenings from October to April anyone can come and gaze at the stars through the observatory's powerful telescope.

☞ Now go straight ahead into Admiral's Walk to the **Admiral's House**, often painted by Constable. In the late 18th century the owner of the house, a naval lieutenant and aspiring admiral, shaped the roof to look like a quarterdeck from where he would fire off a cannon to celebrate the king's birthday. The story inspired the character of Admiral Boom in P.L. Travers's *Mary Poppins*. Sir George Gilbert Scott, architect of St Pancras station and the Albert Memorial, lived here in the 19th century. The lodge next door was later occupied by John Galsworthy, author of *The Forsyte Saga*.

☞ Now return to the crossroads and turn right to Fenton House, which is signposted. On the left just before the gates of Fenton House is New Grove House, former home of George du Maurier, Sir Gerald's father, famous for his *Punch* cartoons and the novel *Trilby*, which introduced both the trilby hat and the character Svengali.

FENTON HOUSE
National Trust • Open Wed-Sun • Charge

This beautiful house, built in 1686, was one of the earliest houses in Hampstead. It is named after merchant Philip Fenton, who bought it in 1793, and was bequeathed to the National Trust by a later owner, Lady Binning, in 1952, along with her collection of porcelain, paintings, needlework and furniture. There are lovely views over London from the top-floor balcony. Fenton House is noted for its collection of early musical instruments donated to the National Trust by Major Benton Fletcher in 1937, which includes a first generation Broadwood piano and a harpsichord made in Antwerp in 1612 and owned by Handel. The instruments are kept in playing condition and are used for lunchtime and evening concerts. The beautiful 300-year-old walled garden features a sunken rose garden and an orchard populated with bees, which produce honey that is available to buy in the shop.

☞ Exit the house and bear right. The white clapperboard house across the green at the bottom was the home and studio of the artist George Romney, while tucked around a corner just beyond is the Holly Bush Inn, a favourite of Dr Johnson's. Cross over and bear left into narrow Mount Vernon, follow it round to the right and then turn left into Holly Walk. Go down Holly Walk, past St Mary's Roman Catholic church, where General de Gaulle worshipped while exiled in London during the Second World War, to . . .

ST JOHN-AT-HAMPSTEAD CHURCH
Open daily • Free

Hampstead's parish church was founded in the 14th century and rebuilt in 1747. Signs in the heavily wooded main churchyard point you to the impressive chest tombs of John Harrison, inventor of the marine chronometer, and artist John Constable. A map available inside the church shows where other famous individuals reflective of Hampstead's artistic and political heritage are buried, such as the comedian Peter Cook, Labour Party leader Hugh Gaitskell, the Llewelyn family of *Peter Pan* fame, architect Norman Shaw, actress Kay Kendall and actor-manager Herbert Beerbohm Tree.

☞ Now walk along Church Row, one of London's handsomest early Georgian streets, and turn left at the end for Hampstead station.

WALK THREE

COLINDALE

One of London's most exhilarating free experiences located on a historic airfield

RAF MUSEUM
Open daily • Free

DIRECTIONS
Exit station, turn left and follow the signs.

Opened in 1972 on the site of the former Hendon Aerodrome, the RAF Museum London tells the story of aviation and of the Royal Air Force. Hendon Aerodrome was one of the world's first aerodromes, established in 1911 by English aviator Claude Grahame-White, the first man to make a night flight. He built a factory there to make aircraft and also ran a flying school, giving flying lessons to, amongst others, author H.G. Wells. The aerodrome can claim a number of aviation firsts. The first air mail flew from Hendon in September 1911, landing at Windsor as part of the celebrations for George V's coronation. In 1912 Hendon hosted the first Aerial Derby around London, attracting some three million visitors. And during the First World War Grahame-White and others mounted a night defence of London from Hendon, the first ever aerial defence of a city. In 1919 Mr Selfridge of the Oxford Street store made the world's first business trip by air from Hendon when he chartered a de Havilland 9 to take him to Dublin.

The Royal Air Force (RAF), founded in 1918, was the world's first independent air force and, at the time, the world's largest air force. The RAF flew out of Hendon and later staged annual air shows there, establishing a connection with Hendon that it maintains today with the RAF Museum. Hendon eventually became too built up for flying operations, which ended there in 1957.

The museum has over 100 historic aircraft and occupies two of the aerodrome's former hangars and three purpose-built exhibition halls. The Milestones of Flight hall traces important events in the history of aviation from the Wright Brothers to the present day. On display here are a 1909 Blériot and a modern Eurofighter. There is also a 3D cinema and Britain's only permanent Air Traffic Control exhibition. Bomber Hall has a Lancaster bomber and a Wellington bomber, one of only two left in the world. The Historic Hangars are a collection of buildings still standing from the old aerodrome and linked together to make a large exhibition space. Here you can see helicopters, aircraft that were modified for flying overseas or landing on water, defensive fighters, such as the world's only complete Hawker Typhoon low interceptor, the only surviving Boulton Paul Defiant night-fighter, and the Allies' first jet fighter, the Gloster Meteor. The Battle of Britain Hall tells the story of the RAF's finest hour, with examples of the aircraft that took part on both sides, including a Spitfire, a Hurricane, a Stuka and a Messerschmitt ME 109. There is also a sound and light show. The Grahame-White Factory, a reconstructed part of the original hangar occupied by Graham-White Aviation, houses the First World War in the Air exhibition, which details the emergence of aviation as a powerful new force in warfare.

North from Camden Town - High Barnet Branch

WALK FOUR

ARCHWAY

Archway is named after the original arched bridge, built in 1813 by John Nash, that took Hornsey Lane over the Great North Road, a little to the north.

A WALK UP HIGHGATE HILL

Taking in a king's love nest and London's most famous tomb

☞ Take the Highgate Hill exit from the station and turn left. Note the pub across the road – this was the Archway Tavern, built in 1888 on the site of a 16th-century inn. Between 1884 and 1909 Europe's first cable-car left from here at the start of its 1½-mile (2.4 km) journey up Highgate Hill to Highgate Village. Alas, we must walk, so continue straight ahead. At the kerbside, just after the Whittington Stone pub on the left, is the **Whittington Stone**. This was placed here in 1821 to mark the spot where Dick Whittington and his cat, heading home to Gloucestershire after failing to make it in London, heard Bow Bells prophesying that their luck would change, and decided to turn back. He subsequently became Lord Mayor of London three (or possibly four) times. The cat was placed here in 1964, a gift from Paul Crosfield whose father, the soap manufacturer

Sir Arthur Crosfield, built Witanhurst at the top of Highgate Hill, the largest private house in London.

☞ Carry on up Highgate Hill, enjoying the fine Georgian architecture, until on your left you come to **St Joseph's Roman Catholic church**. The green copper domes are a well-known north London landmark. It opened in 1889 and has a fabulous Italianate interior that is well worth dropping in to see.

A two-minute diversion along Hornsey Lane, opposite the church, will bring you to the top of the Roman-style Archway bridge, opened in 1897 to replace the original arched bridge designed by Nash. The views of London from here are breathtaking. The bridge soon became known as 'suicide bridge' after a number of people flung themselves off it.

☞ Carry on up Highgate Hill and on your left is the entrance to . . .

LAUDERDALE HOUSE
Open daily • Free

A much restored 16th-century house that now serves as an arts and education centre. Originally a timber-framed house, it was built in 1582 for another thrice Lord Mayor, Sir Richard Martin, and eventually passed into the hands of the Earl of Lauderdale, a friend of Charles II, who allowed the king's mistress Nell Gwyn to live here with her son. It was here that Nell threatened to drop her infant son out of a window unless his father did something for him, provoking the king to cry out in panic, 'Save the Earl of Burford!' The earl ultimately became the Duke of St Albans. The house later served as a boarding house, described by John Wesley, who preached here in 1782, as 'the most elegant boarding house in England'. After many vicissitudes, including fires, the house was saved from dereliction and opened in 1978 as a community exhibition centre and art gallery.

☞ Leave Lauderdale House by the rear entrance into Waterlow Park and follow the signs south-west across the park, making your way between the ponds to the south-west gate. Turn left into Swain's Lane and you are at the entrance to . . .

HIGHGATE CEMETERY
12 minutes ● Open daily ● Charge

If you want a tomb with a view, then come to Highgate Cemetery, which has glorious views over London along with shady avenues, monumental Victorian architecture and a host of illustrious residents. Opened in 1839 as one of the 'Magnificent Seven' (*see* Kensal Green, Bakerloo Line), it was hugely fashionable. The cemetery is divided into two, East and West, both sides being run by the Friends of Highgate Cemetery, but each with different opening arrangements.

East Cemetery. There are guided tours but you can also wander freely through the cemetery on your own, with a map purchased at the gatehouse. Marx and Spencer can be found here, across the main avenue from each other – the revolutionary socialist philosopher Karl Marx and the philosopher Herbert Spencer. Also here are novelist George Eliot, left-wing grandees Paul Foot, Eric Hobsbawm and Ralph Miliband, comedians

Jeremy Beadle and Max Wall, author Douglas Adams, film pioneer William Friese-Greene (*see* Hyde Park Corner, Piccadilly line), punk band manager Malcolm McLaren and actors Corin Redgrave and Sir Ralph Richardson.

West Cemetery. Admission by guided tours only. This less-known, heavily wooded and extremely atmospheric cemetery contains many impressive Victorian architectural features, such as the Chapel, the Terrace Catacombs, the magnificent mausoleum of banker Julius Beer, originally built for his eight-year-old daughter, and the Egyptian Avenue, lined with tombs and leading to the Circle of Lebanon, built around an ancient cedar tree. Buried in the West Cemetery are Beryl Bainbridge, dog-show founder Charles Cruft, Charles Dickens's wife, brother and parents, electricity pioneer Michael Faraday, author John Galsworthy and Alexander Litvinenko, Russian secret agent.

WORKERS OF ALL LANDS
UNITE

☞ Exit the cemetery and follow Swain's Lane downhill to the junction with Chester Road on your left.

Ahead of you, the elaborate Victorian gatehouse is the entrance to **Holly Village**, a self-contained estate of fantastical Victorian Gothic houses built in 1865 by the banking heiress and philanthropist Baroness Burdett-Coutts for her staff. It's private, but you can walk in through the gatehouse and take a look at the meticulously maintained courtyard gardens around which the houses, all turrets and spires and gables, are grouped.

☞ Proceed along Chester Road, following the East Cemetery wall and keep left into Raydon Street, where the wall becomes modern apartments. At the end go left and right into Magdala Avenue. Go to the end, turn right onto Highgate Hill and back to Archway station.

WALK FIVE

FINCHLEY CENTRAL

An inkredible story

STEPHENS HOUSE AND GARDENS
12 minutes • Open daily - house by appointment • Free

DIRECTIONS
Take Station Road exit, turn right into Station Road and left into Regent's Park Road. Keep left at the A504 junction, turn left again into East End Road and the house is on the left-hand side.

Avenue House was built in 1859 and enlarged in 1874 by Henry 'Inky' Stephens, businessman, local MP and son of the inventor of indelible blue-black writing fluid, basis for the famous Stephens' Ink Company, which became a world-wide enterprise selling ink and all kinds of writing materials and equipment. Stephens left the house and grounds to the public on his death in 1918. Located in the conservatory is . . .

THE STEPHENS COLLECTION
12 minutes ● Open Tues, Wed, Thurs afternoons ● Free

The collection examines the life of 'Inky' Stephens and of his father the inventor, the development of Stephens' Ink and the history of writing materials from reeds, clay tablets and papyrus to modern pens, papers and inks.

The gardens were laid out for Stephens by leading landscape architect Robert Marnock and include an arboretum, a rockery, a walled kitchen garden and a quirky statue of Spike Milligan sitting on a bench, entitled *Conversation with Spike*.

South from Camden Town - Charing Cross Branch

WALK SIX

MORNINGTON CRESCENT

ST PANCRAS OLD CHURCH
Open daily • Free

DIRECTIONS
Exit station, turn right and right again and cross the
road into Crowndale Road. St Pancras Old Church is
at the end, on your left, where the road begins to curve.

Here is one of the oldest sites of Christian worship in Britain,
dating back to the early 4th century. Although the present
church was much restored by the Victorians, there are still
fragments of Roman bricks in the fabric, and embedded in the
high altar is a 6th-century Anglo-Saxon altar-stone from an
earlier church, as well as some Norman columns and piers. The
church of St Pancras, which gives its name to the great railway
station next door, was at the heart of a huge country parish
that stretched from what is now Oxford Street up the hill to
Highgate. It became St Pancras Old Church when the centre
of population moved south and the glamorous and expensive St
Pancras New Church, was built in the Greek Revival style, on
the Euston Road in 1822.

The **Old St Pancras churchyard** is now managed by the
council as St Pancras Gardens and contains some interesting

memorials. St Pancras was the last parish church where Roman Catholic mass was said, and Roman Catholics could still be buried there after the Reformation. Many refugees from the French Revolution lie somewhere here and their lost graves are commemorated on a memorial commissioned by philanthropist Angela Burdett-Coutts. This is the first thing you see as you enter the gardens through the iron gates off Pancras Road. Go past this to see the domed tomb of Sir John Soane, designed by himself and the inspiration for Sir Giles Gilbert Scott's famous red telephone box. Around the back of the church is the Hardy Tree, an ash tree surrounded by a mass of headstones placed here by author Thomas Hardy, who as a young architect in the 1860s was tasked with excavating tombs to make way for the construction of St Pancras station.

Others known to have been buried in the churchyard are Johann Christian Bach, known as the London Bach, youngest son of

J.S. Bach, William Franklin, the illegitimate son of Benjamin Franklin, John Flaxman, arguably the greatest ever English sculptor, and early feminist writer Mary Wollstonecraft – it was beside this tomb that poet Percy Bysshe Shelley and his future wife Mary, author of *Frankenstein* and Mary Wollstonecraft's daughter, planned their elopement. St Pancras Gardens provide a magical place of ancient peace amongst the maelstrom of development that is King's Cross.

WALK SEVEN

GOODGE STREET

Toys of yesterday and a glimpse of tomorrow

POLLOCK'S TOY MUSEUM
Open daily • Free

DIRECTIONS
Exit station, turn left and left again into Tottenham Street, then left into Whitfield Street. You will see Pollock's on the right.

You can't really miss Pollock's Toy Shop and Museum on the corner of Whitfield Street and Scala Street. Although it occupies a pair of austere, unrestored back-street Georgian town houses, it is announced to the world by a prancing harlequin on the wall above its gaily painted red and green shop front. Inside all is higgledy-piggledy and cluttered but fascinating, full of toys from another era, from all around the world – dolls and doll's houses, puppets, board games, a Victorian nursery, marbles, train sets, toy theatres, painted wooden building blocks and what is said to be the oldest teddy bear in the world. A creaky, winding staircase takes you up to all kinds of excitements spread over several floors, while the ground floor is a shop.

The collection was started in a small attic room in Monmouth Street by Marguerite Fawdry in 1956, when she bought up all the items she could find left by Benjamin Pollock, the last Victorian toy theatre printer. Added to over the years, the collection soon became too big for the attic and was moved here in 1969.

NEW LONDON ARCHITECTURE
Open Mon-Sat • Free

DIRECTIONS
Exit station, turn right and cross Tottenham Court Road at the first lights to your left. Turn right, cross Chenies Street and take next left into Store Street. NLA is on the right.

NLA is an independent forum for discussion and debate about London's built environment, from planning and development to architecture and construction and the design and impact of new buildings. Here you can see what London may look like in the future with the help of a spectacular giant interactive scale model of central London, including proposed buildings and projects that have been granted planning permission and/or are in development. NLA also showcases new ideas and designs for London and puts on exhibitions, talks, lectures and events.

South from Camden Town - Kennington via Bank

WALK EIGHT

OLD STREET

A methodist mother church and resting place of Puritan authors

WESLEY'S CHAPEL
Open Mon-Sat • Free

DIRECTIONS
Turn left on leaving station and walk down City Road. The chapel is on your left, Bunhill Fields on your right.

This simple, restrained Georgian chapel, designed by George Dance the Younger to John Wesley's plan, and modestly set back from the road, is the 'Cathedral of World Methodism', mother church for more than 70 million Methodists. John Wesley, the founder of Methodism, looks out from the courtyard in front of the chapel, addressing the bustle of 21st-century London with the same vigour and passion he directed at his 18th-century congregation.

The chapel is built on land reclaimed from swamp with material excavated during the building of St Paul's Cathedral. Wesley himself laid the foundation stone in 1777 when he was 74 years old, and the building was opened for worship on 1 November 1778. The chapel was refurbished in 1891 to mark the centenary of Wesley's death. Oak pews were added, stained glass was put in the windows, a new organ was installed and the original oak pillars, gifted by George III and made from ships' masts, were replaced by marble ones given by Methodist congregations from around the world. In 1951 Britain's first female Prime Minister, the late Margaret Thatcher, was married in the chapel, and she later donated the communion rail we see today. By the 1970s the chapel had become neglected and was forced to close, but donations poured in from across the Methodist community and it was reopened by Queen Elizabeth II on 1 November 1978, exactly 200 years after it was first declared open by John Wesley.

At the south side of the chapel is the Foundery Chapel, named after Wesley's very first London chapel, which had been converted from a cannon foundry a few hundred yards up the road. The benches from that first chapel are installed here along with the manual pipe organ belonging to Wesley's famous hymn-writing brother Charles Wesley, who was especially celebrated for the carol 'Hark! The Herald Angels Sing'.

The basement of Wesley's chapel holds a particular treat, the finest surviving Victorian 'gentleman's convenience' to be found anywhere, constructed in 1899 and virtually unchanged since. The lavatory cisterns, or 'valveless water preventers', are by Thomas Crapper, the man who invented the ballcock, and the marble stalls are the work of George Jennings, the man who invented the public lavatory – by charging a penny for those who wished to use his new 'retiring rooms' at the Great Exhibition in 1851 he also gave rise to the phrase 'spend a penny'.

In the chapel crypt is the Museum of Methodism, where you can learn about the history of Methodism and explore its influence in the shaping of Britain's social and political development.

Next door to the chapel is Wesley's House, the delightful Georgian town house where John Wesley lived out the last 11 years of his life. The house is now a museum of his life and contains personal effects and memorabilia, such as his hat and gown, his travelling lamp, the teapot made especially for him by Josiah Wedgwood, and a piece of the tree from Winchelsea in Sussex under which he preached his last open-air sermon in 1790. John Wesley is buried in the memorial garden behind the chapel.

☞ Across the road from Wesley's chapel is . . .

BUNHILL FIELDS BURIAL GROUND

Known as the 'Cemetery for Puritan England', this cemetery was opened in 1665 as a burial site for victims of the plague but it was never consecrated and therefore became a popular burial place for Nonconformists. Prominent amongst those whose graves can be found here are John Bunyan, author of the first English bestseller *The Pilgrim's Progress*, the most read Christian text after the Bible, Daniel Defoe, author of *Robinson Crusoe*, William Blake, author of the words of the anthem 'Jerusalem', and John Wesley's mother Susanna. George Fox, founder of the Quakers, is buried in the adjacent Quaker burial ground.

WALK NINE

LONDON BRIDGE
Also served by Jubilee Line

London's oldest market, highest view, oldest operating theatre, only fashion museum and most historic antiques market

The only Tube station on the network with the name London in it, London Bridge station serves a whole host of well-known south bank riverside attractions. Take the Tooley Street exit and follow signs to the river. Turn left (west) for Southwark Cathedral, London's oldest Gothic church, famous for its lovely 13th-century retrochoir and burial place of Shakespeare's brother Edmund; the Clink, one of Britain's oldest prisons; the Anchor, where Dr Johnson imbibed; Shakespeare's Globe theatre; Tate Modern and the Millennium ('Wobbly') Bridge. Turn right (east) for the shops and restaurants of Hay's Galleria, where most of London's imported dry goods were landed in the 19th century and hence known then as 'the Larder of London'; the Royal Navy's largest ever cruiser HMS *Belfast*; and City Hall. Other places of interest near London Bridge are . . .

BOROUGH MARKET
Open Mon-Sat • Free

DIRECTIONS
Signposted from station.

London's oldest food market Borough Market, at the southern end of London Bridge, was first recorded in the 13th century but almost certainly dates back to Saxon, or even Roman times. Now housed within a Victorian arcade, this colourful maze of passageways and stalls has become fashionable for locally produced fresh produce and international foods of every kind, from breads, pastas and cakes to fish, game, meats, preserves, teas, oils and sweetmeats. This is the market of choice for restaurants and TV chefs.

THE VIEW FROM THE SHARD
Open daily • Charge

DIRECTIONS
Signposted from station.

Towering above London's oldest station is one of the capital's newest attractions, The View from the Shard. This is London's highest viewpoint, 800 feet (244 m) up at the top of the Shard, which at 1,016 feet (310 m) high is the tallest building in the European Union. Brainchild of architect Renzo Piano, the Shard is so called as it is designed to resemble a shard of broken glass. It topped out in 2012 and has proved a highly controversial addition to the London skyline. I am one of those who love it, particularly the way it shimmers and flames as it catches the sun.

The building has 72 habitable floors and houses offices, some of London's highest and most expensive apartments, two hotels and a number of restaurants. The View from the Shard occupies three of the top four floors (68, 69 and 72) and is reached by two lifts, with visitors transferring between lifts on level 33 and exiting at level 68. The journey takes just over one minute and is accompanied by music from the London Symphony Orchestra. Level 69 is a fully enclosed viewing gallery with interactive digital 'Tell:scopes' that provide views of the city in real time as well as showing pre-recordings of the same views taken at different times of the day and night. Level 72 is an open-roofed viewing platform. Both levels offer 360-degree panoramic views of London and on a clear day you can see for up to 40 miles (64 km), beyond the boundaries of Greater London in every direction.

OLD OPERATING THEATRE MUSEUM
Open daily • Charge

DIRECTIONS
Exit main station, turn left and go down the escalator under the Shard. Turn right into St Thomas Street and the entrance to the Operating Theatre is 100 yards (90 m) on the right.

Europe's oldest purpose-built operating theatre was rediscovered in 1956 in a herb garret in the roof of St Thomas's Church, part of the old St Thomas's Hospital. The church was rebuilt in 1703 and the garret was originally used for storing medicinal herbs out of the reach of rats. In 1822 it was kitted out as an operating theatre for women patients and a large skylight was opened up in the roof to provide light. The theatre was built in the roof because it was at the same level as the female hospital wards that were built around it and yet was well sound-proofed and separate enough to prevent infection spreading. The layout of the theatre, with the operating table surrounded by a horseshoe-shaped tiered gallery of seats, illustrates why it was called a theatre – people came to watch, students, apprentice doctors and apothecaries, nurses and even members of the public. The theatre has been restored with original furniture, medical equipment and surgical instruments on display. Gruesome re-enactments are sometimes performed, showing how operations and amputations were done before the days of anaesthetic. Who'd be an actor?

FASHION AND TEXTILE MUSEUM
Open Tues-Sun • Charge

DIRECTIONS
Leave station via the Tooley Street exit, turn right and then next right past the Shipwrights Arms into Bermondsey Street, the high street of fashionable Bermondsey village. The museum is a few minutes' walk away on the left.

Housed in a warehouse converted by Mexican architect Ricardo Legorreta and flamboyantly kitted out in oranges, yellows and pinks, the Fashion and Textile Museum was founded by fashion designer Zandra Rhodes in 2003 and explores all elements of the world of fashion, through textiles, jewellery and design. It has a small permanent exhibition but focuses on regular temporary exhibitions showcasing new talent and ideas and highlighting the importance and influence of past innovators and designers. There are also courses for students and businesses. Chic Bermondsey is a most appropriate place for a fashion museum since the world's very first fashion models came from Bermondsey – six local lasses known as 'Lucile's Mysterious Beauties', who were hired to model clothes at the world's first fashion show, held at Maison Lucile in Hanover Square in 1877.

BERMONDSEY ANTIQUES MARKET

Go to the end of Bermondsey Street, cross over Abbey Street at the zebra crossing, then left, and on your right is Bermondsey Square, home of London's best antiques market, the market that antique dealers come to. More properly known as the New Caledonian Market, having moved here from Caledonian Road in north London in 1948, Bermondsey Antiques Market is held every Friday from 6am.

WALK TEN

MORDEN

Morden is the most southerly Tube station. A short walk further south down London Road is the Baitul Futuh Mosque, opened in 2003 and the largest mosque in Western Europe. There are occasional open days. Morden Park, across the road from the mosque, offers wide views over south London, particularly from the summit where there is a circular pagan burial site.

MORDEN HALL PARK
National Trust • Open daily • Free

DIRECTIONS
Exit station, turn left and then cross the road to your right at the first lights. Turn left and walk to roundabout at the end. Keep right on to Morden Hall Road, cross the road at the lights and the entrance to Morden Hall Park is on your left.

Morden Hall Park, 125 acres (51 ha) of beautiful green space by the River Wandle at the southern end of the Northern line, was formed from the grounds of an ancient manor. Originally the property of Westminster Abbey, the manor was sold at the Dissolution of the Monasteries to Edward Whitchurch, one of the first publishers of the Bible in English. He drained the marshland and built himself a fine Tudor mansion called Growtes beside the river. As a Protestant, he was forced to sell up in 1553 during the reign of Catholic Mary I to the Garth family, who remained at Morden Hall for the next three centuries. In 1770 Richard Garth demolished the Tudor house and replaced it with the Georgian Morden Hall we see today. In 1867 the Hall was sold to the eccentric Hatfeild family, who already ran the well-established snuff mills on the estate, and they were responsible for laying out the gardens more or less as they are now, in particular the huge rose garden and the stable-yard with its splendid clock.

Highlights of Morden Hall Park include nature trails, elegant bridges across the River Wandle, wetlands with wildfowl and kingfishers, a visitor centre in the Stable-Yard, which is said to be the most energy efficient historic building in Britain, and a snuff mill with a restored Victorian water-wheel. The River Wandle once powered over 100 mills, and it was from the snuff produced in mills such as these that the Hatfeilds made their fortune.

Morden Hall itself is run privately as a restaurant and wedding venue.

CHAPTER NINE

The Piccadilly Line

Always, from the first time he went there to see Eros and the lights, that circus have a magnet for him, that circus represent life, that circus is the beginning and the ending of the world

The Lonely Londoners, Samuel Selvon

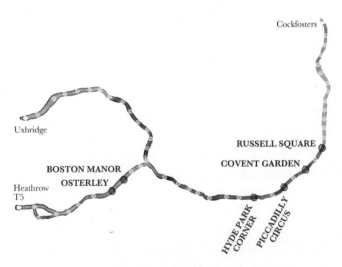

COLOUR: DARK BLUE

YEAR OPENED: 1906

LENGTH: 44 MILES

FASCINATING FACT:

THE JOURNEY OF 284 YARDS (260 M) BETWEEN LEICESTER SQUARE AND COVENT GARDEN STATIONS ON THE PICCADILLY LINE IS THE SHORTEST UNDERGROUND JOURNEY BETWEEN STATIONS ON THE NETWORK AND TAKES ABOUT 20 SECONDS. IT IS THE MOST EXPENSIVE JOURNEY ON THE NETWORK YARD FOR YARD AND YET THE MOST POPULAR

North and east from Piccadilly Circus

WALK ONE

RUSSELL SQUARE

Dickensian London, Britain's first public art gallery, the capital's most unusual artistic venue and a glimpse of the Orient

Russell Square itself takes its name from the family name of the Dukes of Bedford. The square gardens were designed by Humphrey Repton in the early 19th century and restored to their original layout in 2002. The eastern side of the square is dominated by the huge terracotta façade of the Hotel Russell, built in 1898 by Charles Fitzroy Doll, who designed the dining room of the *Titanic* – the dining room of the hotel Russell is said to be a replica.

CHARLES DICKENS MUSEUM
Open daily • Charge

DIRECTIONS

Turn left out of station and immediately left again
into Herbrand Street. Walk to the end (past the Horse
Hospital [*see* below] on your left) and turn left into Guilford
Street. Go past Coram's Fields on your left and Doughty
Mews on your right, and turn right into Doughty
Street. No. 48 is on the left.

Charles Dickens and London are inextricably entwined. London
was his greatest inspiration and he is London's finest chroni-
cler. He created a vision of Victorian London so powerful that
'Dickensian London' is known and recognised all over the world,
and is still how most visitors expect to find London. No. 48
Doughty Street, a typical Georgian terraced house, which
Dickens called 'my house in town', was his first proper house in
London and the only one of his London homes that survives. He
and his new family moved here a year after his marriage in 1837
and remained until 1839, when his increasing wealth enabled a
move to a grander house at Devonshire Place in Marylebone.

The two years Dickens spent at Doughty Street were highly
significant. It was here that two of his daughters, Mary and Kate,
were born and two of his most popular novels, *Oliver Twist* and
Nicholas Nickleby, which established Dickens's reputation as one
of the world's great storytellers, were written in their entirety.
One of the most painful moments of his life also occurred here
when his sister-in-law Mary died in his arms in an upstairs
bedroom at the age of just 17 – the tragedy affected him so
deeply that he actually stopped writing for a while and missed a
number of deadlines. He later drew on his experience with Mary
for describing the death of Little Nell in *The Old Curiosity Shop*.

No. 48 Doughty Street was threatened with demolition in 1923 but was saved by three members of the Dickens Fellowship, a world-wide association of those with an interest in Dickens, who bought and renovated the house and opened it as a museum in 1925. The rooms are laid out in the early Victorian style that Dickens would have known, and personal items, books, portraits, letters and manuscripts are on display throughout the house. The museum now owns over 100,000 items relating to Dickens, the most important collection of Dickens material that exists.

FOUNDLING MUSEUM
Open Tues-Sun • Charge

DIRECTIONS
Turn right out of station, walk to the end of
Bernard Street, cross straight over turn left in
Brunswick Square, then right to museum at the end.

The Foundling Museum stands on the site of the original Foundling Hospital, Britain's very first children's charity, which was established in 1739 by merchant sea captain Thomas Coram as a 'hospital for the maintenance and education of exposed and deserted young children'. Coram invited many of the most illustrious people of the day to contribute to the hospital. Prominent amongst them was William Hogarth, who became a governor and donated a number of his own paintings to the foundation; these, along with works given by Thomas Gainsborough, Sir Joshua Reynolds and Richard Wilson, were displayed at the hospital in what became Britain's first public art gallery. In 1749 George Frideric Handel arranged a special performance of the *Messiah* to pay for the completion of the hospital's chapel – the world's first benefit concert. It was a huge success, attended by the Prince and Princess of Wales, and Handel continued to give a benefit performance of the *Messiah* every year thereafter until his death in 1759.

In 1926 the Foundling Hospital moved out of London to Hertfordshire and the London hospital buildings were demolished, to be replaced in 1935 with the present neo-Georgian structure that now houses the Foundling Museum. On show here is the fabulous collection of paintings, sculptures and artworks given to the foundation over the years, displayed amongst furniture and interiors preserved from the original orphanage, including the splendid rococo Court Room. The story of founder Thomas Coram, the Foundling Hospital, and the artists who supported it, is told in documents and pictures, and there are also many items on show that belonged to the children themselves. On the top floor is the Gerald Coke Handel Collection of manuscripts, printed books and music and other Handel memorabilia – including Handel's will.

A part of the original hospital grounds, Coram's Fields, has been transformed into a playground where no adult can enter unless accompanied by a child.

THE HORSE HOSPITAL
Open Mon-Sat afternoons • Charge

DIRECTIONS
Turn left out of station and immediately left into Herbrand Street. Horse Hospital is 50 yards (45 m) on the left.

Tucked away in a mews behind the station is London's leading independent venue for alternative, underground and avant-garde art, literature, design and film. It was founded in 1992 by production designer Roger Burton and opened with the first retrospective of Vivienne Westwood's punk designs, Vive Le Punk! The gallery aims to provide gallery space to known or unknown artists in an environment free from restrictive rules and etiquette, and encourages unique, innovative and experimental art of the sort that would not normally be exhibited in a conventional gallery. The building that houses the gallery is a work of art in itself: the only surviving unchanged two-floor purpose-built stable open to the public in London. It was built in 1797 by James Burton as a stable for cabbies' sick horses and features a unique herringbone-patterned, mock-cobbled concrete floor. Access to both floors is by a concrete moulded ramp, the upper ramp having hardwood slats to prevent the horses from slipping. On both floors there are original iron pillars with iron tethering rings. This is without doubt one of London's most unconventional and interesting gallery spaces.

BRUNEI GALLERY
Open Tues-Sat ● Free

DIRECTIONS
Turn left out of station, cross ahead into Russell Square. Go to the far (north-west) corner, then right into Thornhaugh Street and immediately left. Entrance to the gallery is on the left opposite SOAS.

Part of the School of Oriental and African Studies (SOAS), the Brunei Gallery is a modern venue for the promotion and presentation of art and culture from Asia, Africa and the Middle East. The gallery puts on regular exhibitions by contemporary artists to supplement the permanent display of the school's huge archive of Asian and African paintings, sculptures and historic artefacts. The gallery was built with an endowment from the Sultan of Brunei and opened in 1995. Visitors can also enjoy peace and quiet in the beautiful Japanese Garden of Forgiveness on the roof, designed as a place for contemplation and meditation.

WALK TWO

COVENT GARDEN

Band cars, trams, trains and buses

Covent Garden Piazza was London's first square, laid out in 1631 by Inigo Jones for the Earl of Bedford. A small fruit, vegetable and flower market quickly established itself on the south side, and when the Earl was granted a royal charter to hold a market in the square, Covent Garden Market blossomed into the biggest and busiest market for flowers, fruit and vegetables in central London. The present market buildings were put up in 1830 and roofed over in 1870. In 1973 the fruit and vegetable market moved south of the river to Nine Elms and Covent Garden reopened as a tourist attraction with stalls, small independent shops, pubs, cafés and restaurants. On the west side of the square is the . . .

LONDON FILM MUSEUM
Open daily • Charge

DIRECTIONS
Exit station and turn right down pedestrianised
James Street to Covent Garden Piazza. Go left, right,
left into Russell Street and first right into Wellington Street.

The London Film Museum, the only museum of its kind in Britain, was opened as the Moviuem of London by photographer Jonathan Sands in 2008. Originally located in County Hall on the South Bank, it moved to Covent Garden in 2012. The museum features original props, costumes and sets from films and television, information on all the major film studios and an exhibition on how films are made. A proud possession is the gong used by the Rank Organisation at the opening of their films. Past highlights have included an exhibition on Charlie Chaplin, featuring his bowler hat and cane, and a display of some of the amazing creatures designed by pioneering special effects expert Ray Harryhausen. In 2014 the Bond in Motion exhibition opened at the museum, featuring many of the vehicles used in the Bond films, including an Aston Martin DB5, the submersible Lotus Esprit from *The Spy Who Loved Me*, Goldfinger's Rolls-Royce Phantom III, and Little Nellie, the gyrocopter from *You Only Live Twice*. Intended as a temporary exhibition, it has proved so popular that it remains at the London Film Museum until further notice.

LONDON TRANSPORT MUSEUM
Open daily • Charge

DIRECTIONS
Exit station and turn right down pedestrianised
James Street to Covent Garden Piazza. Go left and right
and the museum is straight ahead in the south-east
corner of the square.

The story of this museum collection begins way back in the 1920s
when the London General Omnibus Company, London's principal bus operator between 1855 and 1933, decided to preserve
some of its retired buses. Trains, trolleybuses and trams were

later added, and after outgrowing a number of homes around London the collection ended up in the Victorian Flower Market in Covent Garden in 1980. The museum now holds over 450,000 items relating to London's transport history over the past 200 years, with posters, photographs, films, models, memorabilia, and information about how the underground was built, the story of iconic design features, such as the roundel and Harry Beck's map of the London Underground, London's transport during two world wars and visions for future transport possibilities. There are also interactive displays and simulators – you can drive a Northern line train into a station – but the real stars of the museum are the historic vehicles, especially those you can actually climb into. There are horse-drawn buses dating back to 1875 and motor buses from every decade to the present; there are trams dating back to 1882; and there is one of the first steam trains to operate on the first underground railway, the Metropolitan line, in 1866. There is also the very first electric underground train, which dates from 1890 – it had no windows, which were deemed unnecessary since there was nothing to see in the dark. But of course the passengers couldn't see what station they were at either, and so there had to be an announcer at every station, who would run along the carriages shouting out the station name – the ancestors of 'mind the gap'. Hours of fun.

Exhibits for which there is no room at Covent Garden are stored in the Museum Depot, which is open for themed special events and guided tours and is a few minutes' walk from Acton Town station on the Piccadilly and District lines.

WALK THREE

PICCADILLY CIRCUS
Also served by Bakerloo Line

A famous meeting place at the heart of the West End and one of London's busiest spots, Piccadilly Circus comes into its own at night when the neon lights illuminate the bustling crowds congregating to sample the city's nightlife and theatres. The very first product to be advertised in neon here was Bovril, in 1910.

The statue popularly known as Eros (exit 6) is a tribute to the Victorian philanthropist the 7th Earl of Shaftesbury, after whom Shaftesbury Avenue was named. It was unveiled in 1893, the first public statue in the world made of aluminium. On the south-west side of the circus is the Criterion (exit 6), where Dr Watson first heard mention of a potential new flat-mate, 'an eccentric fellow studying at St Bartholomew's Hospital', called Sherlock Holmes; also the celebrated sports retailer Lillywhites, here since 1925, whose No. 5 football was the prototype of the modern football. Lillywhites is now part of the Sports World chain.

On the north side the London Pavilion hosts the world's largest Ripley's Believe It or Not! (exit 4), where you can see a five-legged cow, a picture of Michelle Obama made from bottle tops, the original Toot Sweet machine from the film *Chitty Chitty Bang Bang*, beer made from 5,000-year-old hops found in an ancient Egyptian tomb and some of Marilyn Monroe's personal belongings – amongst other things.

The streets leading off from Piccadilly Circus are home to some of London's oldest and most prestigious shops.

A WALK ALONG PICCADILLY AND JERMYN STREET

☞ Piccadilly takes its name from Piccadilly House, built near here in the 17th century by a merchant called Robert Baker, whose signature product was a type of starched collar known as a 'piccadil'. Walk along the south side (exit 7) and you will soon come to . . .

WATERSTONES

Waterstones' flagship store, the biggest bookstore in Europe, occupies the former home of menswear retailer Simpsons of Piccadilly, for whom the building was commissioned in 1936. It was the first building in London constructed with welded steel. Simpson's was the inspiration for Grace Brothers' department store from the BBC situation comedy *Are You Being Served?* – writer Jeremy Lloyd once worked there. Waterstones hold regular book signings and talks by top international authors, and their 5th View cocktail bar on the fifth floor is a popular meeting place.

☞ Continue along Piccadilly to . . .

ST JAMES'S CHURCH

Consecrated in 1684 and the only one of his London churches built on a completely new site, this was Sir Christopher Wren's favourite. 'I think it may be found beautiful and convenient,' he wrote. The interior is sumptuous, with some wonderful work by Grinling Gibbons, which survived the church being bombed during the Blitz, including the limewood reredos and marble font at which poet and painter William Blake and Prime Minister William Pitt the Elder were baptised. James Gillray the caricaturist is buried here. The church courtyard plays host to Piccadilly Market with stalls selling artworks, crafts, antiques and collectables.

☞ Continue along Piccadilly to . . .

HATCHARDS

Hatchards conforms to almost everyone's idea of what a bookshop should be: five floors of wooden bookshelves, creaking staircases, deep pile carpets, books in every nook and cranny, comfortable chairs, knowledgeable staff and an air of blissful peace. Britain's oldest bookshop was opened in these very premises in 1797 by publisher John Hatchard and quickly attracted a distinguished clientele, wanting to stock the libraries of their big Piccadilly mansions. Amongst those who have browsed its bookshelves are Queen Charlotte, wife of George III, the Duke of Wellington, Lord Byron, William Gladstone, Benjamin Disraeli, Oscar Wilde, Cecil Rhodes and Rudyard Kipling. Hatchards is famous for its huge selection of signed copies, and once or twice a year there are evenings when customers can mingle with the world's top authors as they sign copies of their latest oeuvres.

☞ Next door to Hatchards is . . .

FORTNUM & MASON

London's poshest grocery store Fortnum & Mason was founded in 1707 by Queen Anne's footman William Fortnum and his landlord Hugh Mason. During the Peninsular War they sent out food to the soldiers, and during the Crimean

War, at Queen Victoria's behest, they supplied Florence Nightingale with their celebrated tea. The royal connection is maintained to this day and in 2012 Fortnum's was chosen for the first joint official visit by Queen Elizabeth II, her daughter-in-law the Duchess of Cornwall and her granddaughter-in-law the Duchess of Cambridge. They were each presented with one of Fortnum's trademark hampers, which became popular with Victorian high society for occasions such as Ascot or Henley. Fortnum & Mason has always been innovative. In 1738 Fortnum's staff invented the 'Scotch egg' as a handy portable snack for customers to take with them on the coach journey to their country estates, and in 1886 Fortnum's became the first store in Britain to sell Heinz's canned goods.

☞ Across Piccadilly from Fortnum & Mason is ...

BURLINGTON HOUSE
Open daily • Tours free, charge for exhibitions

The only surviving grand house of the six or seven that lined the north side of Piccadilly in the 17th and 18th centuries, Burlington House was begun in 1664 for Sir John Denham, Charles II's Surveyor of the Office of Works. It was remodelled in the early 18th century for the 3rd Earl of Burlington into one of the first and best Palladian mansions in Britain, and included the first Venetian windows seen in England. In 1854 the house became the property of the government and a few years later the home of the Royal Academy of Arts, which occupies the main house to the north of the courtyard as well as the newer buildings behind, called Burlington Gardens, where most of their temporary exhibitions are held. The buildings on the other three sides of the courtyard are occupied by five other learned societies.

Although the building has been much altered, most of the fine reception rooms in the main house, the first in England to be designed and decorated by William Kent, later added to by Samuel Ware, have survived more or less intact. On 1 July 1858, in the room now known as the Reynolds Room, Charles Darwin and Alfred Russel Wallace presented to the Linnean Society their joint paper on their Theory of Evolution, later made famous by Darwin's *On the Origin of Species*. In 2004 the rooms were restored with funds from the businessman John Madejski, founder of *Auto Trader* magazine, and are now hung with pictures from the Royal Academy's permanent collection. They can be seen when taking one of the regular free tours.

BURLINGTON ARCADE

Britain's first and longest shopping arcade was opened in 1819 for Lord and Lady Cavendish of Burlington House, partly to stop people throwing rubbish into their garden. Lord Cavendish recruited members of his old regiment, the 10th Hussars, to patrol the arcade to make sure that there was no running, whistling, singing or opening of umbrellas, so that his wife and her friends could shop in peace. Known as the Burlington Beadles, they are Britain's oldest police force and still enforce the rules in the arcade today, kitted out in frock-coats and top hats. Hancock's, one of the jewellers in the Burlington Arcade, designed the Victoria Cross medal in 1856. They have produced every VC awarded since.

☞ Now cross back over Piccadilly, turn right and then left down St James's Street. The second building on your left, with the bow window, is . . .

WHITE'S

London's oldest and grandest gentleman's club began life in 1693 as White's Chocolate House, a coffee and chocolate emporium established in Mayfair by Italian immigrant Francesco Bianco (Francis White) and his wife. The rich and raffish of St James's began to congregate there and it soon developed into an exclusive social and gambling club with a notorious reputation – the rake in William Hogarth's *The Rake's Progress* lost his fortune at the gambling tables of White's, as have many real-life characters over the years. White's moved into its present home in 1753 and the bar has never been closed since. In the early 19th century Beau Brummell, friend of the Prince Regent's and arbiter of men's fashion, set up court at a table in the bow window by the front door and this has remained the preserve of only the most senior members ever since. The club's most celebrated bet was made by a member of Beau Brummell's set, Lord Alvanley, who bet on which raindrop would reach the bottom of the bow window first. He was later ruined by his gambling debts and had to resign from the club. Prince Charles and Prince William are both members today, while the Queen is the only woman who has ever been entertained there, in 1991. David Cameron left when he became Leader of the Opposition in 2008, the only person ever to have left White's of his own volition. That's ambition.

☞ Now turn left into Jermyn Street. A little way down on the right is . . .

TURNBULL & ASSER

Shirtmakers to Winston Churchill – they designed his trademark one-piece zip-up 'siren' suit – as well as James Bond and the Prince of Wales, Turnbull & Asser was established in 1885 and moved to these premises in 1903.

TRAMP

At No. 40, on the left, is Tramp, one of London's most exclusive and longest lasting nightclubs. It was founded in 1969 by Brighton bookie Johnny Gold and film producer Oscar Lerman, husband of novelist Jackie Collins, and is named after Charlie Chaplin's character the Little Tramp. Over the years this modest entrance has been a photographic goldmine for the paparazzi. A succession of celebrities, film stars, pop idols and young royals have been snapped staggering out in a dishevelled state after an evening of over-indulgence.

JOHN LOBB

At No. 88 on the right is a branch of John Lobb, Britain's oldest bootmaker, established in 1866 by farmer's boy John Lobb. Crippled by a farming accident, he limped from his home in Cornwall to London to find a job as an apprentice bootmaker with just the aid of a walking stick – lovingly preserved in the John Lobb shop in St James's Street. Turned away for being too scruffy, he went to Australia, set up a successful business in Sydney, married well and returned to London, where he managed to get hold of the Prince of Wales's foot measurements and sent him a pair of boots. The Prince was so impressed that he gave Lobb his Royal Warrant and Lobb never looked back. Shoes are made from individually crafted wooden lasts fashioned to the shape of each customer's feet and Lobb, which is still family run, has lasts belonging to, amongst others, Queen Victoria, Enrico Caruso, Frank Sinatra, Andy Warhol, Laurence Olivier, Harold Macmillan and Prince Charles.

PAXTON & WHITFIELD

Just past John Lobb, at No. 93, is Britain's oldest cheese shop Paxton & Whitfield. In 1742 Stephen Cullum set up a stall in Clare Market in Aldwych selling cheeses shipped to London from around the country – up until then, because of the diffi-culties of transport, cheese had of necessity been eaten near to where it was made. Cullum was so successful he opened a shop and then brought in a partner called Paxton. They were later joined by John Whitfield, and Cullum retired a wealthy man. Paxton & Whitfield, who first brought Stilton to London, gained a Royal Warrant to supply Queen Victoria in 1850, and they moved to their present premises in 1894. They still hold two Royal Warrants, to the Queen and Prince Charles. For anyone who likes cheese, a visit to Paxton & Whitfield is a heady experience.

☞ Go to the end of Jermyn Street and turn left to return to Piccadilly Circus.

South and west from Piccadilly Circus

WALK FOUR

HYDE PARK CORNER

*London's Arc de Triomphe, No. 1 town house
and some hidden rock memorabilia*

Six major roads converge at Hyde Park Corner, once the gateway to London from the west and dubbed the 'busiest corner in the world'. In January 1889 Hyde Park Corner became the second place in the world to appear on moving film (after Leeds Bridge) when pioneer William Friese-Greene set up his experimental box camera at Apsley Gate and shot a length of film featuring 'leisurely pedestrians, open-topped buses and Hansom cabs with trotting horses'.

In the early 19th century architect Decimus Burton designed the massive Hyde Park Corner Screen as a grand entrance to Hyde Park from Buckingham Palace, and visitors still pass through this into the park, at 350 acres (142 ha) the largest open space in central London. In this south-east corner you can find the rose garden, the bandstand, built in 1869 and one of the oldest in Britain, and the Serpentine, a 40-acre (16-ha) lake created by Queen Caroline, wife of George II, in 1730, which provides boating and a lido for swimming.

WELLINGTON ARCH
English Heritage • Open daily • Charge

DIRECTIONS
Signposted from station.

Originally called Constitution Arch and conceived as London's answer to the Arc de Triomphe, the arch was constructed by Decimus Burton in 1828 to be a triumphal entrance to Buckingham Palace, then being remodelled by John Nash for George IV. However, the money ran out and the arch was left *in situ*, bereft of its intended decoration. In 1846 a huge statue of the Duke of Wellington by Matthew Cotes Wyatt, the largest statue ever created, was placed on top of the arch, but by the 1870s Hyde Park Corner had become a traffic bottle-neck and had to be re-designed. The arch was dismantled and moved to its present site, while the much ridiculed statue of Wellington was sent to Aldershot. In 1912 banker Sir Herbert Stern paid for a huge bronze of Adrian Jones's *The Quadriga* to be placed atop the arch in memory of his friend Edward VII, who had admired a smaller version of the sculpture in the Royal Academy. It remains there to this day and is the largest bronze sculpture in Europe. Until the 1950s the arch contained a park keeper's lodge and London's second smallest police station (after the one in Trafalgar Square).

Today, while one half of the arch serves as a ventilation shaft for the underpass, the other half has been opened up to the public with three floors given over to exhibitions, meetings and dining events. There are two open terraces at the top providing surprisingly different views of this part of London, and if you can be there at the right time, you can watch the Household Cavalry marching through the arch beneath you on their way to the Changing of the Guard at Buckingham Palace (*see* Green Park, Victoria Line).

☞ On the north side of Hyde Park Corner is . . .

APSLEY HOUSE
Open Tues-Sun (summer); weekends (winter) • Charge

Apsley House was built in 1778 by Robert Adam for the Lord Chancellor Baron Apsley and was later bought by the Duke of Wellington, victor of Waterloo and instigator of the Wellington boot, in 1817. It became known as 'No.1 London' since it was the first house inside the tollgate on the road into London from the west. Wellington expanded the house but retained many of the Adam interiors, and Apsley House has remained more or less untouched since then. As such it is the only surviving unaltered aristocratic town house of the period in London. In 1947 the 7th Duke gave Apsley House to the nation, while retaining the right of the family to live in an apartment on the second floor 'so long as there is a Duke of Wellington'. The rest of the house was converted for use as a public museum in which to display the 1st Duke's collection of silver, Meissen and Sèvres porcelain, and paintings, many of which are from the Spanish royal collection and were rescued by Wellington from Napoleon after the Battle of Vitoria in Spain and given to him by King Ferdinand. The house has been laid out with furniture belonging to the Duke much as it would have been in his day. Highlights on view include a monumental nude marble statue of Napoleon by Canova, presented to Wellington by the government in 1816, the Waterloo Shield, based on the Shield of Achilles and presented in 1822 and, in the Waterloo Chamber, a re-creation of the dining table set for the Waterloo Banquet, held annually by the Duke for his officers on the anniversary of the battle.

THE VAULT
Open daily • Free – accompanied tours only

DIRECTIONS
Just east of Hyde Park Corner on the corner of Piccadilly and Old Park Lane.

Located in the basement of the Hard Rock Cafe, in what used to be a bank vault belonging to Coutts Bank, is a selection from the world's largest collection of rock memorabilia, donated by musicians and collected by the Hard Rock Cafe from all over the world. The first piece in the collection was Eric Clapton's Fender guitar which Clapton asked to be hung above his favourite seat in the London restaurant to reserve the space for him. Pete Townshend of The Who then did the same, claiming 'Mine's as good as his,' and so it began. Other highlights of the museum include guitars belonging to Jimi Hendrix, Adam Clayton of U2, Lenny Kravitz, Kurt Cobain, Jeff Beck and Slash from Guns N' Roses; Bob Dylan's guitar shaped like a map of the USA; Madonna's pink bustier from her 1990 Blonde Ambition Tour; Eric Clapton's silver suit; John Lennon's glasses and the military jacket he wore on peace marches in the 1970s; Freddie Mercury's favourite antique chair and Elvis Presley's coat.

WALK FIVE

BOSTON MANOR

A hidden Jacobean gem with royal connections

BOSTON MANOR HOUSE
Open weekends • Free

DIRECTIONS
Exit station and turn right. After a few minutes' walk bear right into Boston Manor Park, go past the lake and the house will be in front of you.

A gloriously crooked and comfortable small Jacobean manor house, Boston Manor was built in 1623 for Lady Mary Reade, the young widow of Sir William Reade, stepson to Sir Thomas Gresham and owner of Osterley Park just up the road. Lady Mary was about to remarry, this time Sir Edward Spencer of Althorp, an ancestor of the late Diana, Princess of Wales, and Boston Manor would be their marital home. In 1642, during the Civil War, the staunchly Royalist couple would have been able to watch from the upstairs rooms of the manor house as the Battle of Brentford, a skirmish between Prince Rupert and the Parliamentary forces guarding the western approaches to London, was being fought out in the town on their southern boundary.

In 1670 the house was purchased and extended by City merchant James Clitherow, whose family remained at Boston Manor for the next 250 years, after which the house and grounds were sold to the local council.

The interior of the house is sumptuous, the highlights being the state drawing room on the first floor, which has a magnificent plaster ceiling, and a rare *trompe-l'oeil* balustrade across from the lovely Jacobean oak staircase. Hanging in the bedroom on the first floor are a portrait of Christopher Clitherow by Sir Godfrey Kneller, one of his great-grandson James Clitherow by George Romney and a copy of a portrait of James's sister Jane by Gainsborough, the original of which is in the Frick Collection in New York. The dining room on the ground floor is painted Naples yellow and laid out as it was in 1834 when William IV and Queen Adelaide came to dinner, a rare honour for an untitled family.

The grounds have been laid out as a public park with an ornamental lake and lawns running under the elevated M4 down to the River Brent. This really is a secret world.

WALK SIX

OSTERLEY

A Robert Adam masterpiece amidst London's finest country estate

OSTERLEY PARK
National Trust • Open daily • Charge

DIRECTIONS
Exit station to A4 and turn left. Take first left at lights into Thornbury Road. The gates to Osterley Park are at the end.

Perhaps London's finest surviving country house, Osterley Park belonged originally to banker Sir Thomas Gresham, financial adviser to the Tudors and founder of the Royal Exchange and Gresham College. Gresham purchased the manor in 1562 and replaced the farmhouse already there with a 'faire and stately brick house', known to have been visited by Elizabeth I.

In 1713 the estate was acquired by Francis Child, head of Child's Bank, the bank that introduced the pre-printed cheque (*see* Blackfriars, Circle line); and his grandsons Francis and Robert commissioned two Scottish architects, first Sir William Chambers, and then the newly fashionable Robert Adam, to transform the Tudor mansion into the neo-classical master-piece that we see today. Adam incorporated the Elizabethan towers at each corner of the square courtyard of Gresham's house into his design and created the magnificent colonnaded portico and steps. The Adam interior, according to Adam himself, is 'all delicacy, gaiety, grace and beauty', and some of his finest plasterwork and furniture is on show. Highlights include the Etruscan dressing room, inspired by the Etruscan vases in Sir William Hamilton's collection; the 130 ft (40 m) long gallery; a drawing room 'worthy of Eve before the Fall' according to Horace Walpole, who also referred to Osterley as 'palace of palaces'; and a ceiling by Rubens. The estate eventually passed into the hands of the Earls of Jersey and was given to the National Trust by the 9th Earl in 1949.

The house stands at the centre of a vast park designed largely by Adam but today riven in two by the M4. Gresham's Tudor stables survive, now containing a restaurant and tea shop, along with two lakes, a summer house by Adam and a garden temple by Sir William Chambers – all you could need for a stroll in the country.

On the way between Osterley and the station you will pass the wonderfully eccentric and atmospheric **Osterley Bookshop**, housed in the former ticket office of the old Osterley and Spring Grove station. This 'Jewel in Osterley's Crown', in the words of the *Guardian*, is an unexpected treat, a treasure house of rare and out-of-print books, redolent of the days when the shop sold dairy produce from the cows of Osterley Park and where, even now, you must ring a bell to summon the owner.

CHAPTER TEN

The Victoria Line

Puttin' on the Ritz

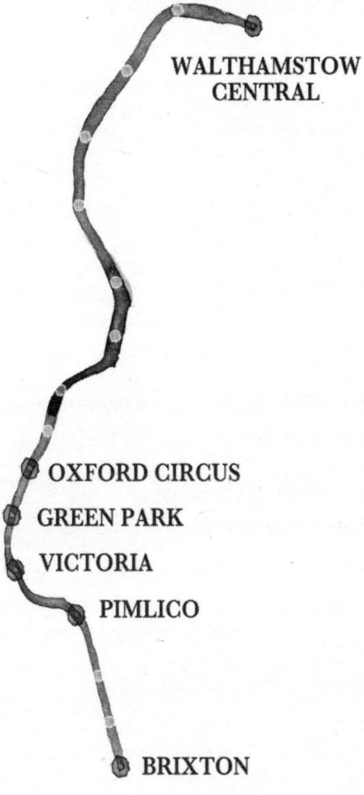

WALTHAMSTOW
CENTRAL

COLOUR: LIGHT BLUE

YEAR OPENED: 1968

LENGTH: 13 MILES

FASCINATING
FACT:

RUNS BETWEEN
TWO OF
LONDON'S MOST
FAMOUS MARKETS,
WALTHAMSTOW IN THE
NORTH AND BRIXTON IN
THE SOUTH

OXFORD CIRCUS

GREEN PARK

VICTORIA

PIMLICO

BRIXTON

North from Victoria

WALK ONE

WALTHAMSTOW CENTRAL

Europe's longest street market, Britain's oldest car and an Arts and Crafts gallery

Given a good plug by the pop band East 17, who not only adopted their home town's post-code as their name (E17) but also called their first album *Walthamstow*, this is nevertheless one of London's less known but most attractive villages. Until the middle of the 19th century Walthamstow was a rural Essex community centred around the 12th-century church of St Mary's, but it then became industrialised and grew into a major commercial and administrative centre. Some picturesque half-timbered old buildings with names such as 'The Ancient House' still survive to help create a villagey feel. Walthamstow is the birthplace of Arts and Crafts designer William Morris, John Kemp Starley, inventor of the modern bicycle, Frederick Bremer, builder of Britain's first petrol-driven motor car, and Andrex lavatory paper, which takes its name from the mill where it was first made in 1932, St Andrew's Mill in the northwest of the district.

WALTHAMSTOW MARKET
Open Tues-Sat • Free

DIRECTIONS
Exit station on to Selborne Road and turn right. At the
top of the road, by the Goose pub, turn left into Hoe Street
for 100 yards (91 m)and the market begins in the
High Street on your left.

Walthamstow Market dates from 1885 and is the longest street
market in Europe, with some 500 stalls stretching almost a mile
along Walthamstow's pedestrianised high street. The market
is open five days a week, Tuesday to Saturday, and trades in
clothing, fabrics, household goods, craft goods and music CDs,
flowers and a range of foods with a particularly good selection
of Caribbean and Asian ingredients. Great fun.

VESTRY HOUSE MUSEUM
Open Wed-Sun • Free

DIRECTIONS
Exit station on to Selborne Road, turn right and go to
the top of the road by the Goose pub. Using the lights
cross straight over Hoe Street. Go straight ahead through
bollards into St Mary Road, and continue along this
road until it narrows into a passageway. Continue
walking until you come out at Church End, and Vestry
House Museum is on your right.

The Vestry House Museum is located in the centre of
Walthamstow Village in the parish workhouse of 1730. A sign
above the door warns 'if any would not work neither should

he eat'. Opened in 1931 the museum explores the history of Walthamstow and displays some of the products manufactured locally, including a wonderful collection of toys and games. There is also a Victorian parlour furnished with Victorian household implements, a costume gallery and the museum's unique and priceless treasure, the Bremer Car, the first car with an internal combustion engine made in Britain. It was built in 1892 by 20-year-old Frederick Bremer, who lived with his family in Connaught Road near the station and put the car together in his workshop in the back garden, using mainly bicycle parts. When he drove the car around the streets of Walthamstow he had to be preceded by a man with a red flag. In 1933 Bremer donated the car to the Vestry House Museum. He died in 1941 and is buried in St Mary's churchyard next door. In 1965 the car completed the London to Brighton veteran car race in eight hours. A thrilling find.

Diversion. If you wish to visit 12th-century St Mary's Church, then turn left on leaving museum and proceed 50 yards (45 m) to the centre of Walthamstow Village, with its Victorian letter box. The Ancient House (15th-century) is on the right and the church on the left. Otherwise, retrace steps and return to Walthamstow Central.

WILLIAM MORRIS GALLERY
12 minutes • Open Wed-Sun • Free

DIRECTIONS
Exit station on to Selborne Road and turn right. At the top of the road, by the Goose, turn left into Hoe Street. Walk along Hoe Street for half a mile (800 m). Just after the brick tower of Goddarts House on the other side of the road, turn left into Ruby Road, following the sign painted high on the wall. Go to the end and you will see the gallery across the road in front of you.

William Morris, designer, leading light in the English Arts and Crafts movement, and socialist campaigner, lived in this gorgeous double bow-fronted Georgian house as a young man from 1848 to 1856. In 1950 the house was declared open by Clement Attlee as a museum dedicated to Morris's life and work, and it now houses the most comprehensive collection of objects related to Morris to be found anywhere, including personal items, such as his satchel and coffee cup. On display are many of his most popular wallpaper designs, stained-glass windows, tiles and wall hangings, one of his first tapestries, the Woodpecker Tapestry, and the *Kelmscott Chaucer*, a richly illustrated copy of the works of Geoffrey Chaucer printed by

Morris's Kelmscott Press. There are also many examples of the work of Morris's friends, particularly Edward Burne-Jones, Dante Gabriel Rossetti and Philip Webb, and others in the Arts and Crafts movement, such as Ernest Gimson, Charles Voysey and Morris's apprentice, Frank Brangwyn.

The grounds of the house have been turned into a public park, with the ancient moat transformed into a series of duck ponds. It was named Lloyd Park after newspaper publisher Edward Lloyd, who bought the house after the Morris family left and whose own family donated the house and park to the people of Walthamstow in 1898.

WALK TWO

GREEN PARK

Also served by Jubilee and Piccadilly Lines

A Royal Collection – or two

The station for Buckingham Palace, London home of the monarch. The palace was begun in 1703 as a house for the Duke of Buckingham and was acquired by George III in 1762 as a private home. George IV asked John Nash to expand the house into a palace and Edward Blore added the familiar east front facing on to the Mall in 1847. Queen Victoria was the first monarch to live there.

The Changing of the Guard takes place on the Palace fore-court at 11.30 daily (except in very wet weather). The State Rooms at Buckingham Palace are open in the summer when the Queen is away at Balmoral. Other parts of the palace are open all year round.

DIRECTIONS

Take Green Park exit and walk south across the park to Buckingham Palace (signposted). You will pass, on your left, Spencer House, London home of the family of the late Diana, Princess of Wales, and one of the finest private palaces ever built in London. Completed in 1766 by James 'Athenian' Stuart, it has the first neo-classical interiors in England and is open to the public for tours on Sundays. For the Queen's Gallery and Royal Mews continue past the palace with the palace forecourt on your right and bear right into Buckingham Gate.

QUEEN'S GALLERY
Open daily • Charge

Opened in 1962 at the west side of Buckingham Palace on the site of a chapel bombed in the Blitz, the gallery exhibits a continually changing selection of artworks from the Royal Collection, formed of works held by the monarch in trust for the nation. Around 450 works are displayed at any one time and include paintings by all the major British and European artists.

ROYAL MEWS
Summer – open daily; winter – Mon-Sat • Charge

The first Royal Mews was located where Trafalgar Square is now and was moved to the rear of Buckingham Palace by George IV in the 1820s. The Mews buildings were designed by John Nash but have been much modified and are today used for stabling the Windsor Greys and Cleveland Bays that pull the royal carriages. Prominent among the carriages housed here is the Gold State Coach, built for George III in 1762. It weighs four tons, requires eight horses to draw it along at walking pace and has been used to carry the monarch at every coronation since George IV in 1821. Also here is the Diamond Jubilee State Coach, built to celebrate the Queen's Diamond Jubilee in 2012 and only the second royal coach to be built in over 100 years. It had its first public outing when carrying the Queen to the State Opening of Parliament in 2014. Garaged at the Royal Mews are the State Cars – two Bentleys, three Daimler limousines and three Rolls-Royces, including a rare Phantom IV, one of only 18 ever made and last seen carrying Prince Charles and Camilla, Duchess of Cornwall, at Prince William's wedding. The Phantom IV was custom built for royalty or heads of state only. You can wander around by yourself with an audio tour or take a free guided tour daily.

☞ To return to Green Park station either retrace your steps across the park or, for a look at some further places of interest, bear right into the Mall as you pass the Queen Victoria Memorial in front of the palace. On the left as you walk along the Mall are Lancaster House, built in 1825 for George III's second son Frederick, Duke of York, and now a government conference centre, and Clarence House, remodelled by John Nash for the Duke of Clarence (later William IV) in 1828 and now home to Prince Charles. It is open for tours in August. Turn left into Marlborough Gate and walk up to St James's Street. On the left is St James's Palace, built for Henry VIII in 1536 and official residence of the monarch since 1698, when Whitehall Palace burned down. The cream painted building on the right is the first classical church in England, the Queen's Chapel, begun by Inigo Jones in 1623 for the aborted marriage of Charles I to the Spanish Infanta, and completed in 1626 for Charles's eventual marriage to Henrietta Maria. Go left and right into St James's Street, past the landmark gatehouse of St James's Palace with its great clock of 1731.

A WALK ALONG ST JAMES'S STREET

On the right walking north (east side) at No. 3 is **Berry Bros & Rudd**, Britain's oldest wine merchant, founded in 1698. Next to it is a passageway leading to **Pickering Place**, the smallest public square in Britain, enclosed by four Georgian brick houses of 1731.

At No. 6 is **Lock & Co** hatters, founded in 1676 and the birthplace in 1849 of the bowler hat.

At No. 9 is **John Lobb**, Britain's oldest bootmaker (*see* Piccadilly Circus, Piccadilly line).

On the left walking north (west side) at No. 71 is **Truefitt & Hill**, the oldest barbershop in the world and barber to the Duke of Edinburgh as well as most male members of the Royal Family since George III. Established in Mayfair in 1805 and moved to these premises in 1994.

Just past No. 64 is the entrance to **Blue Ball Yard**, a beautiful and elegant garden mews of 1742, now part of the Stafford Hotel.

☞ Turn left into Park Place and the first door on the left, painted black, is . . .

Pratt's, a very exclusive dining club started in 1841 by the Duke of Beaufort. He dropped in with some friends on the home of his steward Nathaniel Pratt one evening and had such an enjoyable, convivial time drinking and gaming in the kitchen that he made it a regular event. Members still eat in the kitchen, where there is room for only 14 to dine at one time (out of a membership of 600). All the staff are addressed as George.

On the corner of Park Place and St James's Street at No. 60 is **Brooks's**, founded in 1764 as the headquarters of a group of dandies known as Macaronies because they had developed a taste for macaroni when in Italy on the Grand Tour. They introduced macaroni into England and also invented the word 'bore', meaning someone who isn't a dandy.

Across the street at No. 28 is **Boodle's**, established in 1762 by the Earl of Shelburne, later Prime Minister, and named after the club's first head waiter Edwin Boodle. This was the club to which M, the spymaster in the James Bond novels, belonged, and it is said of Boodle's that if you call out 'Carriage for Sir John' in the smoking room at least a dozen of the members look up.

☞ At the top of St James's Street turn left into Piccadilly and return to Green Park station. You will pass on your left **The Ritz Hotel**, where the Palm Court is the traditional place to take tea. The hotel opened in 1906 and was named after César Ritz, one time manager of the Savoy Hotel. Modelled on the grand French hotels of the period, it was the first hotel in London to have all en suite rooms.

WALK THREE

OXFORD CIRCUS
Also served by Bakerloo and Central Lines

Art deco home of the BBC and Britain's first Victorian High Gothic Church

BBC BROADCASTING HOUSE
Open daily for tours • Charge

DIRECTIONS
Use Oxford Street North Side/Regent Street West Side exit and walk north up Regent Street. Broadcasting House is at the top.

This distinctive art deco building has been the world-wide headquarters of the BBC, the world's first and biggest national broadcasting organisation, since 1932. It originally contained 22 radio studios and the BBC's management offices. The radio mast at the top of the building is a copy of the original mast via which the BBC's radio programmes were broadcast. Above the front door is a sculpture of Ariel, spirit of the air, and Prospero, characters from Shakespeare's *The Tempest* sculpted by Eric Gill, and there are three further depictions of Ariel by Gill at other points on the outside walls. The original building has been modernised and extended, with a new wing added and new studios installed. The new building, known as New Broadcasting House, opened officially in 2013.

There are now 33 radio studios and 14 television studios. The BBC's national stations Radios 1, 3 and 4 broadcast from here, as do the BBC World Service and Asian Network. Radio 2 broadcasts from Western House next door in Portland Street. The BBC News operations moved from Television Centre in Shepherd's Bush into a new state-of-the-art newsroom here in 2013. Most of the BBC's news and political television programmes are now broadcast from here, including the *Daily* and *Sunday Politics* shows, the *Andrew Marr Show* and *Newsnight*, as well as *The One Show*. Visitors can book for a behind-the-scenes tour, which takes in the original art deco reception area, the Media Café overlooking the main newsroom, the Radio Theatre, *The One Show* studio, with a chance to sit on the famous sofa, and the opportunity to have a go at presenting the news or the weather.

All Souls Church next door, with its unique steeple, was designed by John Nash in 1824 as a punctuation point at the top of Regent Street, after planning difficulties had prevented him from completing Regent Street in a straight line northwards to Regent's Park as envisaged in his grand scheme. The church is known for its music and the BBC often broadcasts concerts from there.

ALL SAINTS, MARGARET STREET
Open daily • Free

DIRECTIONS
Use Oxford Street North Side/Regent Street
West Side exit and walk north up Regent Street.
Take second right into Margaret Street and the church
is 200 yards (180 m) along on the left.

One of London's hidden treasures, All Saints is the first, and one of the most beautiful, masterpieces of the High Gothic style of architecture that is so characteristic of the Victorians. Built by William Butterfield between 1850 and 1859, it was the first notable building to use polychrome brick in a decorative way and influenced innumerable churches and public buildings not just in Britain but across Europe for the next fifty years. Apart from its 227 foot (69 m) spire, which still just manages to peek out from above the encircling buildings, the exterior of the church, with its innovative red-and-black banded brickwork, blends into its surrounds and gives no hint of the extraordinary blaze of colour and decoration that greets one inside. Every inch of wall is decorated with richly painted tiles, marble or alabaster. Due to the church's enclosed setting there are few stained-glass windows and no east window – instead the east wall of the chancel is overlaid with gilded panels painted in 1909 by Ninian Comper. The effect is magnificent and overwhelming.

WALK FOUR

VICTORIA
Also served by Circle and District Lines

WESTMINSTER CATHEDRAL
Open daily • Free - charge for tower

DIRECTIONS
Take the main exit from Victoria Station and bear right across the forecourt bus station into Victoria Street. Westminster Cathedral is on the right.

Seat of the Archbishop of Westminster and mother church of the Roman Catholic Church in England and Wales, the Metropolitan Cathedral of the Most Precious Blood was opened in 1903. Somewhat overshadowed by its neighbour Westminster Abbey, Westminster Cathedral is a delightful find. It was designed in neo-Byzantine style by J.F. Bentley and is built entirely of red brick with proportional bands of Portland stone, and with no steel reinforcement. The cathedral inside was incomplete at the time of its opening and internal decoration is still a work in progress. Sir John Betjeman noted that the cathedral looks bigger inside than outside and this is indeed so. The nave is the widest in England, 156 feet (48 m) across and flanked with side chapels, each ablaze with mosaics. On the piers of the nave are the Fourteen Stations of the Cross, carved on limestone by Eric Gill between 1914 and 1918. The walls and columns of the nave are decorated up to half height, above which soaring domes of dark brickwork disappear into blackness. It is an extraordinary effect. The church is also decorated with 126 different kinds of marble from all over the world, the greatest variety of marble in any building in Britain.

There is a small museum of cathedral treasures (entrance charge) and visitors can take a lift to the Viewing Gallery, which is 210 feet (64 m) up near the top of the 273 ft (83 m) high campanile (entrance charge). The view is tremendous and this is one of the least known of London's viewing galleries, which makes for a peaceful and unhurried experience.

South from Victoria

WALK FIVE

PIMLICO

TATE BRITAIN
Open daily • Free

DIRECTIONS
Take the main exit and keep left up the ramp on to Bessborough Street following signs to Tate Britain.

Walk straight ahead and follow the road left to Vauxhall
Bridge Road. Cross at the lights, turn right and left at the
lights into John Islip Street. Continue across two side streets
and then turn right through the black iron gates marked
'university of the arts london'. This was once the Royal Army
Medical College where the vaccine for typhoid was developed
in 1897, and is now the Chelsea College of Art and Design.
Veer left across the Parade Ground, which today is used for
exhibitions as London's largest open air gallery, and Tate
Britain is ahead of you.

This, the original Tate Gallery, was opened in 1897 as somewhere to showcase the finest of British art. It was funded by
sugar magnate Sir Henry Tate, who donated his own collection
of British paintings to form a nucleus for the early displays. A
large part of the gallery's collection of modern art was transferred to Tate Modern downstream on Bankside when it
opened in 2000, and the gallery here was renamed Tate Britain.
Tate Britain still owns the largest collection of British art in the
world, dating from 1500 to the present, and the largest collection of works by J.M.W. Turner. The gallery puts on regular
temporary exhibitions while on permanent display are paintings by Hogarth, Gainsborough, Millais, Joshua Reynolds,
Stubbs and William Blake, while more modern artists are
represented by Stanley Spencer, Henry Moore, Francis Bacon,
Lucian Freud and Damien Hirst. Highlights include John
Constable's *Flatford Mill*, Millais's *Ophelia*, Whistler's *Nocturne:
Blue and Gold – Old Battersea Bridge*, John William Waterhouse's
The Lady of Shalott and Turner's *Norham Castle*.

WALK SIX

BRIXTON

Britain's first department store, the world's first electrically illuminated market and the nearest windmill to London Bridge

Brixton is edgy, arty and vibrant with a big African and Caribbean population, lots of trendy nightclubs and a growing population of young up-and-coming professionals. It is the birthplace of, amongst others, David Bowie, Max Wall, Sharon Osborne and the department store. In 1877 printer James Smith, fresh from watching his racehorse Roseberry win both the Cesarewitch and the Cambridgeshire Stakes at Newmarket, spent his winnings on putting up London's first purpose-built department store on Brixton Road, which he called Bon Marché after the original Paris store. After 40 years of successful trading it became a Selfridges store, then a John Lewis, before becoming derelict, and is now a business centre. Look to your right as you exit the station onto Brixton Road, and the Bon Marché building, identified by a masonry sign high up on the roof, is a short way down on the other side of the road, just beyond the two railway bridges.

BRIXTON MARKET

Exit Brixton station and turn left then left again into Electric Avenue, which in the 1880s became the first market street in the world to be lit by electricity – and in the 1980s gave its name to a hit single by Eddy Grant. You are now in the heart of Brixton

Market, a street market established in the mid-19th century and famous for its selection of foods from around the world – Indian, Asian, African, South American and Caribbean. The covered arcades and railway arches that surround the street market are full of cafés, restaurants and shops and together form Brixton Village.

BRIXTON WINDMILL
15 minutes • Second Sunday in the month April - October •
Pre-booked tours • Free

DIRECTIONS
Exit station, go straight across Brixton Road using
the pedestrian lights and turn left. Go straight over
Acre Lane and continue along Brixton Hill, keeping the
town hall on your right. At the fourth set of traffic
lights turn right into Blenheim Gardens. The windmill
is at the end.

The nearest windmill to central London, Brixton windmill was built in 1816 for local millers Ashby & Sons, taking the name Ashby's Mill. At the time this was open fields and the mill was used for grinding up corn until 1862, when the area had begun to get built up around it and there was no longer enough wind to drive the sails. The Ashbys moved to a new water-mill on the River Wandle but in 1902 moved back to Brixton and installed a steam engine to power the mill and later a gas-powered engine. They continued to grind corn here until 1934, when the mill closed and fell derelict. For the next 70 years the story of the windmill was one of partial restoration

and further neglect until 2003, when local residents formed the Friends of Windmill Gardens and began a campaign to save and restore the mill. In 2016, two hundred years after it was first built, Brixton windmill began producing stoneground flour again and selling it in Brixton Market. The mill is open from April to October with open access to the first floor, while the second floor is open for pre-booked guided tours only. Windmill Gardens host outdoor events in summer.

CHAPTER ELEVEN

The Docklands Light Railway

The greatest view in Europe
      Sir Christopher Wren on the view of Greenwich
                                    from the Isle of Dogs

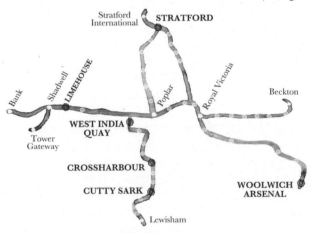

COLOUR: TURQUOISE

YEAR OPENED: 1987

LENGTH: 25 MILES

FASCINATING FACT:

THE DLR WAS BRITAIN'S FIRST DRIVERLESS RAILWAY
SYSTEM. CANARY WHARF DLR STATION IS THE BUSIEST
STATION ON THE UNDERGROUND MAP THAT IS SERVED
BY ONLY ONE LINE

WALK ONE

LIMEHOUSE

Canal-side walk and museum

Limehouse takes its name from the many lime kilns that operated here from the 14th century onwards, burning chalk brought up the river from Kent to produce lime for London's building industry. The area was famous in the 19th century for its opium dens – Sherlock Holmes visited one looking for clues in *The Man with the Twisted Lip* – and Limehouse was the setting for Sax Rohmer's stories about Dr Fu Manchu, modelled on a Chinese man the author bumped into on Limehouse Causeway on a foggy night in 1911.

RAGGED SCHOOL MUSEUM
Open Wed-Thurs • Free

DIRECTIONS

Exit the station, turn right and proceed east along Commercial Road. After 100 yards (90 m) you will cross the canal. Take the steps on your left down to the towpath and walk north for a few minutes until you pass under the railway bridge. Shortly after that you will see signs to the museum, located in a canal-side warehouse.

Located in the very warehouse that once housed Dr Thomas Barnardo's largest 'ragged' or free school, the Ragged School Museum tells the story of the poor children of the East End of London in Victorian days and of the doctor who made it his mission in life to help them. Thomas Barnardo came to London from Dublin in 1866, with the intention of studying medicine at the London Hospital and then becoming a missionary in China. He found an East End that was overcrowded and rife with poverty and disease. Not long after he arrived the area was struck by an outbreak of cholera, which left thousands of children orphaned and destitute, and Barnardo determined to help them. In 1867 he set up his first ragged school where children could get a free education, and in 1870 his first home for boys, in Stepney Causeway. On one occasion an 11-year-old boy nicknamed 'Carrots' was turned away from the home because it was full and two days later he was found dead of exposure. After that Dr Barnardo made his famous vow – 'No Destitute

Child Ever Refused Admission'. In 1873 Barnardo opened a home for girls in Barkingside, and by the time of his death in 1905 there were 96 Dr Barnardo's homes looking after more than 8,500 children.

Barnardo's Copperfield Road Free School operated until 1908, by which time there were enough government schools to provide education for the local children. The warehouse was then used for a number of industrial purposes until, in the 1980s, it was threatened with demolition. Local people rallied round to save their heritage and the Ragged School Museum opened in 1990. Inside they have recreated a Victorian classroom where you can sit at the desks and enjoy a Victorian school lesson, and a Victorian East End kitchen filled with Victorian kitchen utensils – should the mood take you, you can even experience a bath in a tin bathtub.

WALK TWO

WEST INDIA QUAY

London's docks and fishy tales

MUSEUM OF LONDON DOCKLANDS

Open daily • Free

DIRECTIONS

Signposted from station.

Located in a group of early 19th-century sugar warehouses beside West India Dock, this museum, part of the Museum of London, explores the history of London as a port from

Roman times to the present, focusing on London's Docklands and London's relationship with the River Thames. Since the 1980s Docklands has been going through the largest regeneration project in Europe and the museum sits at the centre of it, reflecting the changes that have been made since the closure of the central London docks in 1980. There are 12 galleries arranged in chronological order over three floors, with a children's gallery called Mudlarks on the ground floor. Floor 3 covers the Thames Highway from the founding of London in AD 43 to 1800; Floor 2 covers the 19th century, when London was the biggest port in the world, used by over half of all the world's merchant ships; Floor 1 displays documents, photographs, objects, films and sound recordings from the archive of the Port of London Authority, which charts the history of London's port and docks from the 1770s.

BILLINGSGATE FISH MARKET
Open Tues-Sat, 4-9.30am • Free

DIRECTIONS
Signposted from station.

Like London's port, London's fish market, which received its charter from Edward III in 1327, was the biggest in the world in the 19th century. At that time it stood next to the City of London's main wharf, beside the water gate called Billingsgate after Belinus, a legendary king of the Britons, who is said to have erected London's first water gate. In 1982 the fish market moved down river to its present location on the Isle of Dogs. Covering some 13 acres (5.3 ha), it is Britain's largest inland fish market both in size and in terms of the daily selection of fish, 60 per cent of it coming from British ports. Although Billingsgate is primarily a wholesale market, anyone can go there to buy fish, or just for the experience, provided they can get up early enough (it is open from 4am to 9.30am) and you can be assured of the best, freshest and widest selection of fish in the capital – for anyone keen on fresh fish Billingsgate is paradise. There are also guided tours available for those who wish to go behind the scenes and experience the unique atmosphere, bustle, cries and the smells of Billingsgate (*see* website on page 314 for tours).

WALK THREE

CROSSHARBOUR

MUDCHUTE FARM
Open daily • Free

DIRECTIONS
Exit station, walk directly across the road and through the
ASDA car park. The entrance to Mudchute Park and
Farm is at the far right-hand side.

Here is London's largest urban farm, one of the largest in
Europe, set in 32 acres (13 ha) of meadows and wetland on
the southern tip of the Isle of Dogs. It is a working farm with a
huge variety of different farm animals and provides a glimpse of
the countryside in the heart of the city. There are rare Dexter
cows, Gloucestershire Old Spots, the oldest breed of spotted
pig in the world, adorable pot-bellied pigs, three varieties of
sheep, goats, two donkeys, mother and daughter, llamas and
alpacas, ducks, chickens, geese and turkeys and a Pets Corner
where you can cuddle rabbits, guinea pigs, ferrets and some
surprisingly adorable 'Dumbo' rats. There is also a riding
school. Tramping through green fields and woodlands full of
wild flowers and enjoying farmyard sounds and smells while in
the shadow of the towers of Canary Wharf is a marvellously
surreal experience.

WALK FOUR

CUTTY SARK

Go from west to east for fine architecture and views, the world's only fan museum and a world-class art collection

Greenwich, where East meets West, is the birthplace of three Tudor monarchs, Henry VIII, Mary I and Elizabeth I, the setting for one of the most beautiful architectural vistas in the world, Sir Christopher Wren's favourite, and a World Heritage Site brimming over with places of interest. Here you can see the last remaining tea clipper in the world, the fully restored *Cutty Sark*; the biggest painting in Britain, the ceiling of the Painted Hall, completed over 20 years by Sir James Thornhill; Britain's first Palladian house, the Queen's House, designed by Inigo Jones and completed in 1635; as well as the world's largest maritime museum, London's oldest royal park, enclosed in 1427, the Royal Observatory, the Prime Meridian and one of London's liveliest markets. Also not to be missed is . . .

THE FAN MUSEUM
Open Tues-Sun • Charge

DIRECTIONS
Exit station and turn left into the alleyway with Waterstones
on your left, then turn right, away from the *Cutty Sark*, into
the main street. Go straight ahead at the lights with the
entrance to Greenwich Market across the road on your left
and continue to Nicolas Hawksmoor's St Alfege Church,
where Thomas Tallis, the father of English church music,
and General Wolfe, the hero of the Battle of Quebec,
are buried. After the road bends to the right cross over
to your left and go straight ahead into Stockwell Street.
You will soon see the Greenwich Theatre on your left,
and the Fan Museum is opposite at the end of the
Georgian terrace.

If you want to escape for a moment from the tourist trails, then
this unique place, the only fan museum in the world, offers a
delightful respite. Housed in two charming early 18th-century
houses, it owns the largest collection of fans in the world, more
than 4,000 of them, dating from the 12th century to the present
day and gathered together from all around the world. The
museum was opened in 1991 by Richard and Helene Alexander
and most of the fans are from Helene's own collection, but it
has also been gifted or bequeathed fans and is always on the
lookout for further acquisitions. The heyday of the fan was the
18th and 19th centuries, and there are many fine examples from
this period when the fan was not just an accessory but a status
symbol and a work of art. There is also a fine collection of art
deco fans, fans used as advertising tools and some quirkier fans,
such as one that can be worn as a bonnet.

Looking through the museum is a little like wandering around a particularly colourful art gallery. There is a permanent exhibition in two ground-floor rooms devoted to the history of the fan and the art of fan making. Here you can see a fan leaf painted with a depiction of the Grand Dauphin's 20th birthday celebrations from the court of Louis XIV in the late 17th century, a fan-shaped painting called *Landscape in Martinique* painted by Paul Gauguin in 1887, and a fan painted by Walter Sickert from the 1890s showing Little Dot Hetherington on stage at the old Bedford Theatre. Not all the fans can be shown at one time, so the assortment on display is changed three times a year and there are temporary exhibitions based on different themes. These in the past have included Waterloo, Life and Times, with fans celebrating the bicentenary of the Battle of Waterloo; Visions of Beauty, with fans showing depictions of mythical goddesses and contemporary beauties; and Curiosities and Quirky Fans – with curious and quirky fans. There are also regular workshops, tea in the Orangery and a garden at the back with a fan-shaped parterre.

RANGER'S HOUSE AND THE WERNHER COLLECTION

English Heritage • Restricted opening – pre-booked guided tours only • Twice daily Sun-Wed • Charge

DIRECTIONS

As for the Fan Museum. Then continue up Crooms Hill for another ten minutes with Greenwich Park on your left and some glorious Georgian houses on your right. Go past the tollgate at the top and shortly you will see Ranger's House on your left. If you return through

the park, you will be able to enjoy one of London's
favourite views from the statue of General Wolfe and
also straddle the hemispheres in the courtyard of
Flamsteed House, starting point of the
Prime Meridian.

Here you can see one of the world's finest private art collections
displayed in one of London's finest Queen Anne mansions with
one of London's finest views. The house was built in 1699 for
Vice Admiral Francis Hosier, one of many naval officers to
make himself a home at Greenwich, the centre of Britain's maritime activity, from where he could keep an eye on the Thames.
It then came into the possession of the Earl of Chesterfield who
added the east wing, now the Chesterfield Gallery, in which
to house his art collection.

To restore symmetry to
the house an almost iden-
tical west wing was added by
a subsequent owner, Richard
Hulse of the Hudson's Bay
Company, in the 1780s. In 1815
the house became a royal grace and
favour home for a niece of George
III, Princess Sophia Matilda, who
became the first resident Ranger
of Greenwich Park (a royal
park), and the house was given
the name Ranger's House. The
last Ranger left in 1896 and since
then the house has been used as a

tea room, a barracks, a local exhibition centre and offices. In 1986 English Heritage took over and refurbished the house as a home for the Wernher Collection, made up of over 700 works of art assembled by Sir Julius Wernher, who made his fortune in the diamond mines of Kimberley in South Africa.

The collection, which includes furniture, carvings, sculptures, ceramics, pottery, porcelain, jewellery and Renaissance bronzes, as well as paintings, was originally on show at Luton Hoo, Wernher's home in Bedfordshire, but when that was sold in the 1990s the collection was leased to English Heritage and put on display in Ranger's House. Three particularly notable items are a painting of the view over London from Crooms Hill in the 19th century by Thomas Christopher Hofland, which shows how it would have then looked from Ranger's House; a life-like terra-cotta bust of George IV's Queen Caroline (a former Ranger) when she was Princess of Wales by Anne Seymour Damer, in which the mistreated consort appears surprisingly attractive; and a stunning life-size marble sculpture by Giulio Bergonzoli called *The Love of Angels*, which is displayed in the bow window.

WALK FIVE

WOOLWICH ARSENAL

Keeping your powder dry

ROYAL ARSENAL

Free

As well as possessing Britain's longest unbroken Georgian façade – the 1,060 ft (323 m) long south face of the Royal Artillery Barracks – and being the birthplace of Britain's first building society, the Woolwich, in 1844, and Arsenal Football Club in 1886, and the site of Britain's first McDonalds in 1974, Woolwich has been home to the Royal Arsenal since Henry VIII set up an ordnance depot at Woolwich Dockyard in the first half of the 16th century.

Amongst the first guns held at Woolwich were those captured from the Spanish by Sir Francis Drake. At first Woolwich was just used to store guns and gunpowder, but then in 1695 the Royal Laboratory was moved there as a safe location to manufacture such things as gunpowder, shell cases, fuses and gun cartridges. The Royal Regiment of Artillery was formed in 1716 under the command of the Board of Ordnance to guard the arsenal, and the Royal Engineers a year later to provide engineering and technical support to the army. (A gun foundry was established in 1717 and a gun carriage works in 1750.) The arsenal expanded hugely during the Napoleonic Wars, was named the Royal Arsenal by George III in 1805 and slowly grew into one of Britain's largest and most innovative manufacturing works, covering some 13,000 acres (5,250 ha) by the start of the First World War and employing 80,000 workers. At one time the Royal Arsenal was so top secret that it wasn't even marked on the A-Z and just appeared as a mysterious blank by the waterfront. After the Second World War, as the nature of warfare and ordnance changed, different elements of the Royal Arsenal began to close down or move away, and Woolwich ceased to be a military site altogether in 1994. Today the arsenal site is being rebuilt for industrial and residential use. Some of the more notable historic military buildings have been retained and converted for other uses. At the heart of the complex, in Artillery Square, is the . . .

GREENWICH HERITAGE CENTRE
Open Tues-Sat • Free

This museum tells the story of Greenwich, England's first royal dockyard, and of Woolwich and the Royal Arsenal since Roman times. There are displays and exhibitions of a wide range of archaeological material and artefacts with maps, photographs and paintings. The museum also holds some parts of the collection of the world's oldest military museum, the Royal Artillery Museum, which used to be on the site, and includes an exhibition on the history of artillery, examples of some very early weaponry, some 16th-century iron cannons, guns from the 17th and 18th century, items recovered from the *Mary Rose*, uniforms, diaries and medals, articles related to campaigns in which the Royal Artillery has participated, and interactive displays that recreate the experience of being under fire.

WALK SIX

STRATFORD
Also served by Central, Jubilee and Overground Lines

The Olympic spirit and Britain's tallest sculpture

Home to the largest urban shopping centre in the European Union, one of London's most famous theatres, the Theatre Royal Stratford East, and the 2012 Olympics Games, once gritty Stratford has undergone a massive regeneration project in the last 20 years and is now an internationally known tourist destination. At the heart of it all is the . . .

QUEEN ELIZABETH OLYMPIC PARK
Open daily • Free

DIRECTIONS
Signposted from station.

London's newest park, a lasting legacy of the 2012 Olympic Games and one of the largest urban parks created anywhere in Europe since Victorian times, offers a mix of sporting facilities, parkland, wetlands and canal-side walks and nature trails. There is swimming at the London Aquatics Centre, a public gym in the Copper Box Arena, tennis courts, cycling in the VeloPark and various walking trails through the 560 acres (227 ha) of park. These including an art trail past the public artworks commissioned for the Olympics, the London 2012 trail that takes in the sites of the Games, and a trail that explores the park's history and fauna and wildlife. The best place to get an overview is from the top of the . . .

ARCELORMITTAL ORBIT
Open daily • Charge

At 376 feet (114 m) this is Britain's tallest sculpture and largest piece of public art – and a great new way of seeing London from a different perspective. Described variously as 'a fusion between striking art and daring engineering' and 'the Godzilla of public art', it was designed by Indian-born sculptor Sir Anish Kapoor, engineered by Arup and largely paid for by steel tycoon Lakshmi Mittal. It is certainly 'a genuine eyecatcher'. There are two indoor viewing platforms, the upper one 262 feet (80 m) up, both offering unique views of the Olympic Park and across

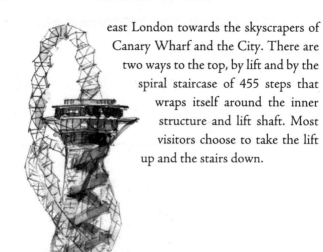

east London towards the skyscrapers of Canary Wharf and the City. There are two ways to the top, by lift and by the spiral staircase of 455 steps that wraps itself around the inner structure and lift shaft. Most visitors choose to take the lift up and the stairs down.

CHAPTER TWELVE

Overground

A thing of beauty is a joy for ever

'Endymion', John Keats

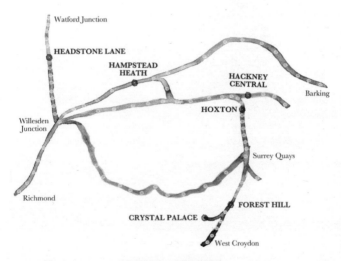

COLOUR: ORANGE

YEAR OPENED: 2007 (AS LONDON OVERGROUND)

LENGTH: 53.4 MILES

FASCINATING FACT:

THE EAST LONDON LINE SECTION OF THE OVERGROUND
RUNS THROUGH THE WORLD'S FIRST MAJOR
UNDERWATER TUNNEL, THE THAMES TUNNEL
BETWEEN WAPPING AND ROTHERHITHE

Euston to Watford Junction Branch

WALK ONE

HEADSTONE LANE

Museum centred on moated 14th-century manor house

HARROW MUSEUM

12 minutes • Open Wed-Sun • Free

DIRECTIONS

Exit station, turn left and follow Headstone Lane
down the slope. Walk for a few minutes and you will
see a brown sign pointing left to Harrow Museum,
which is in the middle of the park.

The star of Harrow Museum is Headstone Manor, a glorious,
rambling timber-framed building dating from 1310. The

oldest house in Middlesex, it features superb work from the 14th, 17th and 18th centuries and sits in the middle of one of the only complete, filled moats in London, constructed at the same time as the earliest part of the house. The land was part of the ancient manor of Harrow, owned by a Middlesex nobleman called Wulfred who was Archbishop of Canterbury at the beginning of the 9th century. The land stayed with the archbishops and Headstone Manor became one of their most important residences. In 1546, after the Dissolution of the Monasteries, Thomas Cranmer gave the manor to Henry VIII, who sold it on to one of his court lawyers, Baron North. For the next 400 years the house was occupied by tenant farmers and slowly fell into a state of neglect before being saved by local campaigners in the 1980s and restored.

The manor house is the centrepiece of a unique complex of historic buildings, which includes a Great Barn of 1506, made of English oak, a smaller barn dating back to the 14th century when the manor house was built, and an 18th-century granary moved here from nearby Pinner Park Farm. Each of the buildings contains a selection of museum exhibits, covering the history of the local area from Roman times to the present with particular emphasis on Harrow's industrial heritage. The quiet garden setting is delightful and the museum makes for a good country day out from London.

North London Line - Stratford Branch

WALK TWO

HAMPSTEAD HEATH

The poet Keats's last home and the National Trust's first Modernist house

The station sits on the southern edge of Hampstead Heath, 790 acres (320 ha) of woodlands, meadows, ponds and wildlife, the largest area of common land in London and one of the best places in the city for any type of walk from a gentle stroll to an energetic hike. Parliament Hill, a steepish 15-minute walk from Hampstead Heath station, is 322 (98 m) above sea level and has glorious views over London – the view of the Houses of Parliament from the summit is one of London's 13 protected views. 17th-century Kenwood House on the north side of the park is about 35 minutes' walk from the station and offers gardens, a concert bowl, a splendid Robert Adam library and a fine collection of paintings. This was once the London home of the Lord Chief Justice, the 1st Earl of Mansfield, and the setting for the famous painting of his great nieces Dido Elizabeth Belle and Lady Elizabeth Murray, that inspired the 2013 film *Belle*. The Earl's deep affection and respect for Belle is thought to have contributed to the radical rulings he made in cases involving slavery that began the move towards Abolition.

George Orwell lived near Hampstead Heath station in 1934–5, above Booklover's Corner, the bookshop where he worked, on the corner of South End Road and Pond Street. There is a plaque to this effect on the building, which is 100 yards (90 m) left and left again out of the station and on the right at the corner. It is now a Le Pain Quotidien bakery. While lodging there Orwell wrote *Keep the Aspidistra Flying*. In 1935 he moved to 77 Parliament Hill, on the other side of the station.

If you go straight out of the station and turn right on South Hill Park you come almost immediately to the Magdala pub, outside which Ruth Ellis, the last woman to be hanged in Britain, shot dead her boyfriend David Blakely in April 1955. You can still see the bullet marks. Coincidentally, the second to last woman to be hanged in Britain, Styllou Christofi, committed the murder for which she was executed a little further along in the same street, at 11 South Hill Park, nine months before in July 1954.

KEATS HOUSE

Open Summer Tues-Sun afternoons ● Open winter Fri-Sun afternoons ● Charge

O for a beaker full of the warm South!
Full of the true, the blushful Hippocrene
'Ode to a Nightingale', John Keats

DIRECTIONS

Turn left out of station and use the zebra crossing ahead of you to cross South End Road. Turn right, walk ahead past the shops, allowing time for a browse in Daunt Books, turn left into Keats Grove and Keats House is on the left after 100 yards (90 m).

John Keats lived here from 1818 to 1820 and this is where he wrote some of his finest poetry – in particular five of his six great odes, including 'Ode to a Grecian Urn' and 'Ode to a Nightingale'. The house was newly built, one of the first to be put up in this part of Hampstead, and was in fact two houses, semi-detached with a shared garden and then called Wentworth Place. Charles Wentworth Dilke, the liberal critic and antiquary, lived in the larger house while the poet Charles Brown occupied the smaller abode. Brown invited Keats to come and lodge with him after Keats's brother Tom, with whom Keats had lived nearby in Well Walk, died of consumption. The following year Dilke moved away from next door and let the house to a widow, Mrs Brawne, and her family, who took up residence in April 1819. Keats would often walk in the garden with one of the daughters, Fanny Brawne, and they inevitably fell in love and became engaged – secretly, as an impoverished poet was not considered a good match. Keats soon became too weak with tuberculosis to venture outside, having caught a chill while travelling on the outside of a coach to save money, and they had to communicate solely by letter, although Fanny was later allowed to nurse the invalid poet. In September 1820 Keats sailed for the warmer climes of Italy, knowing he would probably never see Fanny again, and indeed he died in Rome in February 1821.

In 1838 an actress, Eliza Chester, bought both houses and knocked them into one, adding a drawing room to the eastern end. In the 1920s the house was going to be knocked down to make way for a block of flats, but money was raised to rescue the property and maintain it as a memorial to Keats. Today the house is managed by the City of London and run as a museum to the life and works of John Keats and his fiancée Fanny Brawne. The house is laid out as in Keats's day with displays of memorabilia, such as Keats's letters to Fanny, some of the books he wrote his poetry in, Charles Brown's copy of Keats's *Endymion* ('A thing of beauty is a joy for ever') and items of Fanny Brawne's jewellery, including her engagement ring from Keats and a medallion containing a lock of Keats's hair. Visitors can wander in the gardens where Keats walked with Fanny and see the mulberry tree beneath which, according to Charles Brown, Keats wrote 'Ode to a Nightingale'.

2 WILLOW ROAD
National Trust ● Open Wed-Sun ● Charge

DIRECTIONS
Take same directions as for Keats House but instead
of turning left into Keats Grove continue along
South End Road, bear left into the dead-end road,
continue to the end, cross over and straight on into
Willow Road. No. 2 is 50 yards (45 m) on the left.

The first Modernist house acquired by the National Trust (in 1993) and one of only two Modernist houses in England open to the public, 2 Willow Road was designed as a home for himself and his family by the Hungarian-born architect Erno Goldfinger in 1939. The terrace of three houses, set in a quiet, leafy side street, is made of concrete, faced with red brick, and was built against much opposition from local residents, who thought it out of keeping with the neighbourhood. One particularly vociferous critic was the James Bond author,

Ian Fleming, who later got his revenge by naming one of his most notorious villains after the architect – Auric Goldfinger.

No. 2 is the largest of the three houses, has a central spiral staircase created by the Danish engineer Ove Arup and is filled with furniture designed by Goldfinger himself. Goldfinger was very much a 'Hampstead intellectual', one of a group of left-wing artists and thinkers who lived in Hampstead in the 1930s, and 2 Willow Road is full of works by liberal artists, such as Henry Moore, Barbara Hepworth and Roland Penrose, many bought at an 'Aid to Russia' auction Goldfinger held at Willow Road in 1942.

WALK THREE

HACKNEY CENTRAL

SUTTON HOUSE
National Trust ● Open Wed-Sun ● Charge

DIRECTIONS
Exit station, cross over at the lights in front of you to your left, then right and left into Mare Street. Cross over to St John's churchyard and walk through it, keeping the walled garden on your left. At the far side walk ahead into Sutton Place, lined with Georgian houses, go to the end and Sutton House is on your right.

Originally called the Bryck Place, Sutton House is the second oldest brick house in London after Bromley Hall in Bow. It was built in 1535 for Ralph Sadler, protégé of Thomas Cromwell and Secretary of State to Henry VIII, and is mistakenly named after Thomas Sutton, founder of Charterhouse (*see* Barbican,

Hammersmith & City), who in fact lived next door. Over the years the house was home to merchants, sea captains, Huguenot weavers, General Picton, the most senior officer to die at the Battle of Waterloo, school teachers, clergymen, union boss Clive Jenkins and, in the 1980s, squatters. All have left their mark, although behind the Georgian exterior this is essentially still a Tudor house, with the rooms of Tudor linen-fold panelling, oak carved windows and fireplaces all beautifully restored and laid out in Tudor décor to give an impression of life in a Tudor household. A highlight is the oldest private loo in London, a brick alcove fitted with a lead pipe built as part of the original house in 1535. There is also a small museum of local history, atmospheric evening tours and late night film events and concerts.

East London Line

WALK FOUR

HOXTON

GEFFRYE MUSEUM
Open Tues-Sun • Free

DIRECTIONS
Hoxton station overlooks the back of the museum.
Go down Cremer Street keeping the museum on
your right and turn right on Kingsland Road for
the entrance.

For those in the know this museum is a favourite, exploring the way of life of England's middle classes through their living rooms. Eleven rooms are laid out in period decoration and furnishings dating from 1600 to the present day. Each room has its own atmosphere and reflects the changes in society, taste and fashion as the middle class emerges and gets richer. As you progress chronologically from the bare, basic but homely rooms of the 17th century, ornaments and pictures begin to appear, new methods of heating and lighting are developed, furniture becomes simpler, less ornate, rooms become more cluttered with gadgets, radios, televisions. The rooms also change with the season; Christmas is particularly revealing, with very little festive decoration until the 19th-century rooms when Christmas trees and cards begin to bloom – the legacy of the Hanoverians and later Charles Dickens. The detail is immaculate and every room is absorbing – you will find you have spent far more time here than you anticipated, almost literally lost in another world.

The museum is named after Lord Mayor of London Sir Robert Geffrye and housed in a beautifully restored set of almshouses built for the Ironmongers' Company, of which he was master, in 1714. The gardens are laid out in different periods as well, providing further insight into changing lifestyles and social conditions.

WALK FIVE

FOREST HILL

London's most eclectic private collection and the world's first purpose-built art gallery

HORNIMAN MUSEUM
Open daily • Free

DIRECTIONS
Exit station, turn left and cross the road to your right at lights. Go straight ahead on London Road (following brown signs to Horniman Museum and Gardens) and after a few minutes you will see the Horniman Museum clock tower ahead of you on the right.

Set in 16 acres (6.5 ha) of landscaped gardens, the Horniman Museum opened to the public in 1901 and is one of London's most popular attractions. At its core is the vast array of anthropological and natural history specimens, cultural artefacts and musical instruments collected on his travels by Frank Horniman, owner of what was then the world's largest tea trading company. His desire was to 'bring the world to Forest Hill', and at first he put everything on display in his home, Surrey Mount, and invited the public in to have a look. The house quickly became too small and so Horniman had it demolished and replaced by an art nouveau museum designed by Charles Harrison Townsend. He then donated the museum and grounds to the London County Council as a gift to the people of London.

Today the collection has grown from some 30,000 items to over 350,000, and highlights include a huge stuffed walrus from Hudson's Bay, over 130 years old, a Japanese mermaid, a torture chair, a dinosaur footprint, ancient Egyptian mummies and coffins, 16th-century virginals and a wealth of objects that can be handled and experienced. There are regular workshops, exhibitions and events and also an aquarium, a remarkable Victorian conservatory, a small animals enclosure, a nature trail, a sound garden where you can play large musical instruments and a 100-year-old bandstand with spectacular views over London.

At the museum's entrance stands a 20 ft (6 m) high totem pole carved in 1985, and on the outside wall of the main building is a mosaic mural of various figures depicting aspects of the human condition.

DULWICH PICTURE GALLERY
25 minutes • Open Tues-Sun • Charge

Soane has taught us how to display paintings

Architect Philip Johnson

DIRECTIONS
As to the Horniman Museum. Then carry on along
London Road leaving Horniman on your right. At
second set of traffic lights, just past church with tall
spire on the left, cross road to your left and walk ahead on
Dulwich Common. When you come to the gates of
Dulwich Park on your right, enter the park and bear
left on the main path. Follow this, keeping the
boating lake on your right, and at the end of a short
stretch of road with parked cars you will see the
Picture Gallery straight ahead of you.

The world's first purpose-built public art gallery, Dulwich
opened in 1817 and contains one of the world's finest collections of Old Masters. It all began in 1790 with French art dealer
Noël Desenfans and his friend, the Swiss painter Sir Francis
Bourgeois, who were commissioned by the King of Poland,
Stanislaus Augustus, to gather together a royal collection. By
the time they had acquired the paintings, mostly the work of

17th- and 18th-century European artists, the king had been forced to abdicate and the collection was eventually donated to Dulwich College, on the condition the pictures were made available for the public to see. The college already had a small number of paintings left by founder Edward Alleyn, and as there were now nearly 400 pictures in the combined collection it was decided to build a special public gallery in which to show them. This was designed by leading architect Sir John Soane, who pioneered the use of skylights to allow in natural light to illuminate the paintings. Dulwich Picture Gallery has ever since served as a model for art galleries all over the world.

The number of paintings at Dulwich is now over 600, with a particularly fine collection of European masterpieces. Highlights include Sir Joshua Reynolds's portrait of the actress Sarah Siddons, Thomas Gainsborough's *The Linley Sisters*, Rembrandt's *Girl at a Window*, and Nicolas Poussin's *The Triumph of David*.

Incorporated in the gallery buildings is a mausoleum where the founders of the collection, Sir Francis Bourgeois and Noël Desenfans, are buried.

Dulwich Park is particularly lovely in spring and summer when its famous displays of azaleas and rhododendrons are flowering. Dulwich Village, the northern extension of the street on which the picture gallery is located, is also very pretty, lined with Georgian houses, cafés and shops, and is worth a gentle stroll along if you still have the time and energy.

WALK SIX

CRYSTAL PALACE

CRYSTAL PALACE PARK
Open daily • Free

The Crystal Palace, Sir Joseph Paxton's magnificent iron and glass exhibition hall, which had first been erected in Hyde Park for the 1851 Great Exhibition, was rebuilt on Sydenham Ridge and opened in 1854 as the centrepiece of a 200-acre (81 ha) pleasure park. In 1911 the Festival of Empire was held here in celebration of the coronation of George V. The Crystal Palace burned down in 1936 in a spectacular conflagration that attracted thousands of sightseers, after which the park suffered many years of neglect, but it has since been much restored.

Over the years the park developed as a sporting venue with the establishment of Crystal Palace Athletics Club in 1868. Cricketer W.G. Grace based his London County Cricket Club at Crystal Palace and would walk across the road from his house 'Parklands', located north of the park, to play. The FA Cup final was played on the football ground here between 1895 and 1914, and in 1905 it became the first home of Crystal Palace Football Club (now moved to nearby Selhurst Park). The ground is today the site of the National Sports Centre, Britain's first multi-use sports park, which opened in 1964.

In 1868 the world's first air show was held at Crystal Palace, made up of working models of airships and contemporary flying machines, and in 1902 Britain's first airship, Stanley Spencer's Airship No. 1, left from Crystal Palace on its maiden flight, landing in Highgate. In 1928 one of the world's first speedway tracks opened at Crystal Palace. This developed into the Crystal Palace motor-racing circuit where many of the great Grand Prix drivers raced. The circuit closed in 1972 but since 2010 sections of the track have been used for sprint and time trials during the annual May bank holiday 'Motorsport at the Palace' event.

☞ Turn left out of the station to the site of the Crystal Palace itself. Situated in the former Crystal Palace School of Engineering, the only building left after the fire of 1936, is the ...

CRYSTAL PALACE MUSEUM
Open weekends • Admission free

The museum tells the story of the Crystal Palace with photographs, documents and some pieces salvaged from the fire. Beyond are the grand Italian terraces upon which the Crystal Palace stood, and you can still climb one of the sweeping staircases on to the terraces to look out over London. The BBC TV and radio transmitter at the north end of the terraces is 719 ft (219 m) high and was once the highest structure in London.

In the middle of the park, near the central car park, which is overlooked by a bust of Sir Joseph Paxton unveiled in 1873, is the Tea Maze, 160 feet (49 m) in diameter and the largest maze in London. Laid out in 1870, it was so named as being a popular place to visit after tea.

In the south-east corner of the park (turn right out of the station), scattered around the 'tidal lake', are 33 full-sized models of prehistoric animals, the **Crystal Palace Dinosaurs**. They were constructed in 1854 by Benjamin Waterhouse Hawkins, illustrator of Charles Darwin's account of the voyage of the *Beagle*, under the guidance of Professor Richard Owen, the leading scientific expert of the then newly discovered world of prehistoric creatures and inventor of the word 'dinosaur'. These were the first representations of dinosaurs the public had ever seen and they caused a sensation.

Gazetteer

Bakerloo Line

Kensal Green Cemetery, Harrow Road, London W10
Tel: 020 8969 0152 www.kensalgreencemetery.com

BAPS Shri Swaminarayan Mandir, London, 105–119
Brentfield Road, London NW10
Tel: 020 8965 2651 www.londonmandir.baps.org

London Zoo, Regent's Park, London NW1
Tel: 020 7449 6200 www.zsl.org/zsl-london-zoo

The National Gallery, Trafalgar Square, London WC2
Tel: 020 7747 2885 www.nationalgallery.org.uk

The National Portrait Gallery, St Martin's Place, London WC2
Tel: 020 7306 0055 www.npg.org.uk

British Optical Association Museum, 41-42 Craven Street,
London WC2
Tel: 020 7766 4353
www.college-optometrists.org/en/college/museyeum

Benjamin Franklin House, 36 Craven Street, London WC2
Tel: 020 7925 1405 www.benjaminfranklinhouse.org

Household Cavalry Museum, Horse Guards, Whitehall SW1
Tel: 020 7930 3070 www.householdcavalrymuseum.co.uk

Morley Art Gallery, 61 Westminster Bridge Road, London SE1
Tel: 020 7450 1826 www.morleycollege.ac.uk/morley_gallery

St George's Cathedral, Westminster Bridge Road,
London SE1
Tel: 020 7928 5256 www.stgeorgescathedral.org.uk

Imperial War Museum, Lambeth Road, London SE1
Tel: 020 7416 5000 www.iwm.org.uk

Garden Museum, 5 Lambeth Palace Road, London SE1
Tel: 020 7401 8865 www.gardenmuseum.org.uk

Florence Nightingale Museum, 2 Lambeth Palace Road,
London SE1
Tel: 020 7620 0374 www.florence-nightingale.co.uk

Cinema Museum, 2 Dugard Way, London SE11
Tel: 020 7840 2200 www.cinemamuseum.org.uk

Central Line

Tyburn Convent, 8-9 Hyde Park Place, London W2
Tel: 020 7723 7262 www.tyburnconvent.org.uk

Pitzhanger Manor, Walpole Park, Mattock Lane, London W5
Tel: 020 8567 1227 www.pitzhanger.org.uk

Ealing Studios, Ealing Green, London W5
Tel: 020 8567 6655 www.ealingstudios.com

British Museum, Great Russell Street, London WC1
Tel: 020 7323 8299 www.britishmuseum.org

Museum of Comedy, The Undercroft, St George's Church,
Bloomsbury Way, London WC1
Tel: 020 7534 1744 www.museumofcomedy.com

Cartoon Museum, 35 Little Russell Street, London WC1
Tel: 020 7580 8155 www.cartoonmuseum.org

James Smith and Sons, Hazelwood House, 53 New Oxford
Street, London, WC1
Tel: 020 7836 4731 www.james-smith.co.uk

St Giles-in-the-Fields, 60 St Giles High Street, London, WC2
Tel: 020 7240 2532 stgilesonline.org

Foyles, 107 Charing Cross Road, London, WC2
Tel: 020 7437 5660 www.foyles.co.uk

Gay Hussar, 2 Greek Street, London. W1
Tel: 020 7437 0973 gayhussar.co.uk

The House of St Barnabas, 1 Greek Street, London, W1
Tel: 020 7437 1894 hosb.org.uk

Soane Museum, 13 Lincoln's Inn Fields, London WC2
Tel: 020 7405 2107 www.soane.org

Lincoln's Inn, Newman's Row, London WC2
Tel: 020 7405 1393 www.lincolnsinn.org.uk

Hunterian Museum, The Royal College of Surgeons, 35-43
Lincoln's Inn Fields, London WC2
Tel: 020 7869 6560 www. hunterianmuseum.org

Old Curiosity Shop, 13-14 Portsmouth Street, London, WC2
Tel: 020 7405 9891

Cittie of Yorke, 22 High Holborn, London, WC1
Tel: 020 7242 7670

London Silver Vaults, Chancery House, 53-64 Chancery Lane,
London WC2
Tel: 020 7242 3844 www.silvervaultslondon.com

Ede & Ravenscroft, 93 Chancery Lane, London, WC2
www.edeandravenscroft.com

Barnard's Inn Hall, Holborn, London EC1
Tel: 020 7831 0575 www.gresham.ac.uk/barnards-inn-hall

Museum of Childhood, Cambridge Heath Road, London E2
Tel: 020 8983 5200 www.vam.ac.uk/moc

Circle Line

The Monument, Fish Street Hill, London EC3
Tel: 020 7626 2717 www.themonument.info

St Bride's Church, Fleet Street, London EC4
Tel: 020 7427 0133 www.stbrides.com

Dr Johnson's House, 17 Gough Square, London EC4
Tel: 020 7353 3745 www.drjohnsonshouse.org

Temple Inns of Court, Middle Temple Lane, London, EC4
Tel: 020 7427 4820 www.middletemplehall.org.uk

Twinings Museum, 216 Strand, London WC2
Tel: 020 7353 3511
www.twinings.co.uk/about-twinings/216-strand

Royal Courts of Justice, Strand, London WC2
Tel: 07789 751248 (for pre-booked tours)
www.justice.gov.uk/courts/rcj-rolls-building/rcj/tours

Courtauld Gallery, Somerset House, Strand, London WC2
Tel: 020 7848 2526 www.courtauld.ac.uk/gallery

Savoy Chapel, Savoy Hill, London WC2
Tel: 020 7836 7221 www.royalchapelsavoy.org

Westminster Abbey Chapter House and Pyx Chamber,
Dean's Yard, Westminster Abbey, London SW1
Tel: 020 7654 4900 www.english-heritage.org.uk/visit/places/
chapter-house-and-pyx-chamber

The Jewel Tower, Abingdon Street, London, Westminster,
London SW1
Tel: 020 7222 2219 www.english-heritage.org.uk/visit/places/
jewel-tower

Churchill War Rooms, Clive Steps, King Charles Street,
London SW1
Tel: 020 7930 6961 www.iwm.org.uk/visits/churchill-war-
rooms

Guards Museum, Wellington Barracks, Birdcage Walk,
London SW1
Tel: 020 7414 3271 www.theguardsmuseum.com

Museum of Music, Royal College of Music, Prince Consort Road, London SW7
Tel: 020 7591 4300 www.rcm.ac.uk/museum

Design Museum, Kensington High Street, London W8 (from 2016)
www.designmuseum.org/about-the-museum/design-museum-kensington

Leighton House Museum, 12 Holland Park Road, London W14
Tel: 020 7602 3316
www.rbkc.gov.uk/subsites/museums/leightonhousemuseum1.aspx

Linley Sambourne's House, 18 Stafford Terrace, London W8
Tel: 020 7602 3316
www.rbkc.gov.uk/subsites/museums/18staffordterrace1.aspx

District Line

Fulham Palace, Bishop's Avenue, London SW6
Tel: 020 7736 3233 www.fulhampalace.org

St Mary's Church, Putney High Street, London SW15
Tel: 020 8394 6061 www.stmarys.parishofputney.com

Wimbledon Lawn Tennis Museum, Church Road, Wimbledon, London SW19
Tel: 020 8788 4414 www.wimbledon.com/en_GB/museum_and_tours

Chiswick House, Burlington Lane, Chiswick, London W4
Tel: 0370 333 1181
www.english-heritage.org.uk/visit/places/chiswick-house

Hogarth's House, Hogarth Lane, Great West Road, London W4
Tel: 020 8994 6757
www.hounslow.info/arts-culture/historic-houses-museums/
hogarth-house

St Nicholas Church, Chiswick Mall, London, W4
Tel: 020 8995 7876 www.stnicholaschiswick.org

Fuller's Brewery, Great Chertsey Road, Great West Road,
London W4
Tel: 020 8996 2000 www.fullers.co.uk/brewery/book-a-tour

London Museum of Water and Steam, Green Dragon Lane,
Brentford, Middlesex TW8
Tel: 020 8568 4757 www.waterandsteam.org.uk

The Musical Museum, 399 High Street, Brentford,
Middlesex TW8
Tel: 020 8560 8108 www.musicalmuseum.co.uk

Kew Gardens, Kew, Richmond, Surrey, TW9
Tel: 020 8332 5655 www.kew.org

Whitechapel Gallery, 77-82 Whitechapel High Street, London E1
Tel: 020 7522 7888 www.whitechapelgallery.org

Whitechapel Bell Foundry, 32-34 Whitechapel Road, London E1
Tel: 020 7247 2599 www.whitechapelbellfoundry.co.uk

Royal London Hospital Museum, St Augustine with St Philip's
Church, Newark Street, London E1
Tel: 020 7377 7608 www.bartshealth.nhs.uk/about-us/museums,
-history-and-archives/the-royal-london-museum

Three Mills, The Miller's House, Three Mill Lane, London E3
Tel: 020 8980 4626 www.housemill.org.uk

Barking Abbey, Sandringham Road, Barking, Essex, IG11
Tel: 020 8594 2932 historicengland.org.uk

Eastbury Manor, Eastbury Square, Barking, Essex IG11
Tel: 020 8227 2942 www.nationaltrust.org.uk/eastbury-manor-house

Hammersmith & City Line

Museum of Brands, Packaging and Advertising, Lighthouse
Building, 111-117 Lancaster Road, London W11
Tel: 020 7908 0880 www.museumofbrands.com

The Magic Circle Museum, 12 Stephenson Way, London NW1
Tel: 020 7387 2222
venue.themagiccircle.co.uk/submenus/rooms/the-museum/

Wellcome Collection, 183 Euston Road, London NW1
Tel: 020 7611 2222 www.wellcomecollection.org

University College London, Gower Street, London WC1
Tel: 020 7679 2000 www.ucl.ac.uk

Flaxman Gallery, Octagon Gallery, UCL, Gower Street
entrance, London WC1 Tel: 020 7679 2000
www.ucl.ac.uk/museums/uclart/about/collections/john-flaxman

Jeremy Bentham auto-icon, South Cloisters, UCL, Gower
Street, London WC1
www.ucl.ac.uk/museums/jeremy-bentham

Grant Museum of Zoology, Rockefeller Building, UCL,
21 University Street, London WC1
Tel: 020 3108 2052 www.ucl.ac.uk/museums/zoology

Petrie Museum of Egyptian Archaeology, Malet Place,
London WC1
Tel: 020 7679 2884 www.ucl.ac.uk/museums/petrie

Church of Christ the King, Gordon Square, London, WC1
www.forwardinfaith.com/EnglishChapel.php

Kings Cross and St Pancras Station and Hotel, Euston Road,
London, NW1
www.marriott.co.uk/hotels/travel/lonpr-st-pancras-renaissance-
hotel-london

London Canal Museum, 12-13 New Wharf Road, London N1
Tel: 020 7713 0836 www.canalmuseum.org.uk

British Library, 96 Euston Road, London NW1
Tel: 0330 333 1144 www.bl.uk

The Charterhouse, Charterhouse Square, London EC1
Tel: 020 7253 9503 www.thecharterhouse.org

St Bartholomew's Hospital Museum, West Smithfield,
London EC1
Tel: 020 3465 5798 www.bartshealth.nhs.uk/bartsmuseum

Priory Church of St Bartholomew the Great, West Smithfield,
London EC1
Tel: 020 7600 0440 www.greatstbarts.com/

Museum of London, 150 London Wall, London EC2
Tel: 020 7001 9844 www.museumoflondon.org.uk/london-wall

Barbican Arts Centre, Silk Street, London EC2
Tel: 020 7266 7000 www.barbican.org.uk

Jubilee Line

Abbey Road Studios, 3 Abbey Road, London NW8
Tel: 020 7266 7000 www.abbeyroad.com/

Lord's Cricket Ground, Grace Gate, St John's Wood Road,
London NW8
Tel: 020 7616 8500
www.lords.org/lords/things-to-do/tours-of-lords

MCC Museum, Grace Gate, St John's Wood Road, London NW8
Tel: 020 7616 8658
www.lords.org/history/mcc-museum-library-and-collections/
mcc-museum

The Stables Gallery and Art Centre, Gladstone Park, Dollis
Hill Lane, London NW2
Tel: 020 8452 8655 www.brentarts.org.uk

St Lawrence's Church, Whitchurch Lane, Edgware,
Middlesex HA8
Tel: 020 8952 0019 www.little-stanmore.org

Bentley Priory, Mansion House Drive, Stanmore HA7
Tel: 020 8950 5526 www.bentleypriory.org

Wallace Collection, Hertford House, Manchester Square,
London W1
Tel: 020 7563 9500 www.wallacecollection.org

Kirkaldy Testing Museum, 99 Southwark Street, London SE1
Tel: 01604 838111 www.testingmuseum.org.uk

St Mary's Church, 72A St. Marychurch Street, Rotherhithe,
SE16
Tel: 020 7394 3394 www.stmaryrotherhithe.org/

Mayflower Pub, 117 Rotherhithe Street, London SE16
Tel: 020 7237 4088 www.mayflowerpub.co.uk/

The Rotherhithe Picture Research Library, 82 St. Marychurch
Street, Rotherhithe, London SE16
Tel: 020 7231 2209 www.sandsfilms.co.uk/Sands_Films_
Studio/Rotherhithe_Picture_Library.html

Brunel Museum, Railway Avenue, Rotherhithe, London SE16
Tel: 020 7231 3840 www.brunel-museum.org.uk

The O2 or Millennium Dome, Peninsula Square, London SE10
Tel: 020 8463 2000
www.theo2.co.uk/do-more-at-the-o2/up-at-the-o2

Emirates Aviation Experience, Edmund Halley Way,
London SE10
Tel: 020 3440 7021 www.aviation-experience.com

Emirates Air Line
www.emiratesairline.co.uk

Metropolitan Line

Sherlock Holmes Museum, 221b Baker Street, London NW1
Tel: 020 7224 3688 www.sherlock-holmes.co.uk

Madame Tussauds, Marylebone Road, London NW1
Tel: 0871 894 3000 www.madametussauds.com/London

Royal Academy of Music Museum, Marylebone Road,
London NW1
Tel: 020 7873 7373 www.ram.ac.uk/museum

St Marylebone Church, 17 Marylebone Road, London NW1
Tel: 020 7935 7315 www.stmarylebone.org

St Etheldreda's Church, 14 Ely Place, London EC1
Tel: 020 7405 1061 www.stetheldreda.com/

St Peter's Italian Church, 136 Clerkenwell Rd, London EC1
Tel: 020 7837 1528 www.italianchurch.org.uk

Marx Memorial Library, 37A Clerkenwell Green, London EC1
Tel: 020 7253 1485 www.marx-memorial-library.org

St James's Church, Clerkenwell Cl, London EC1
Tel: 020 7251 1190 http://www.jc-church.org/

St John's Church, St John's Gate, London, EC1
Tel: 020 7324 4005 www.museumstjohn.org.uk

Museum of the Order of St John, St John's Lane,
Clerkenwell, London EC1
Tel: 020 7324 4005 www.museumstjohn.org.uk

Freud Museum, 20 Maresfield Gardens, London NW3
Tel: 020 7435 2002 www.freud.org.uk

SSE Arena, Arena Square, Engineers Way, London HA9
Tel: 020 8782 5566 www.ssearena.co.uk

Wembley Stadium, Wembley, London HA9
Tel: 0844 980 8001 www.wembleystadium.com

St Martin's Church, Eastcote Rd, Ruislip HA4
Tel: 01895 625456 www.stmartins-ruislip.org/

Manor Farm, Bury Street, Ruislip, Middlesex HA4
Tel: 01895 558234 www.hillingdon.gov.uk/manorfarm

The Battle of Britain Bunker, RAF Uxbridge, Uxbridge, UB10
Tel: 01895 238154 www.raf.mod.uk/battleofbritainbunker

Heath Robinson Museum, West House, West End Lane,
Pinner, HA5
heathrobinson.org/museum

Three Rivers Museum, Basing House, 46 High Street,
Rickmansworth, Herts WD3
Tel: 01923 727333 www.trmt.org.uk

Rickmansworth Waterways Trust, 99 Church Street,
Rickmansworth, Herts WD3
Tel: 01923 778382 www.rwt.org.uk

Northern Line

Burgh House, New End Square, London NW3
Tel: 020 7431 0144 www.burghhouse.org.uk

Fenton House, Hampstead Grove, London NW3
Tel: 020 7435 3471 www.nationaltrust.org.uk/fenton-house

St John-at-Hampstead Church, Church Row, London NW3
Tel: 020 7794 5808 www.hampsteadparishchurch.org.uk

RAF Museum, Grahame Park Way, London NW9
Tel: 020 8205 2266 www.rafmuseum.org.uk/london

Lauderdale House, Waterlow Park, Highgate Hill, London N6
Tel: 020 8348 8716 www.lauderdalehouse.co.uk

Highgate Cemetery, Swain's Lane, London N6
Tel: 020 8340 1834 www.highgatecemetery.org

Stephens House, 17 East End Road, London N3
www.stephenshouseandgardens.com

The Stephens Collection, 17 E End Road, London, N3
Tel: 020 8346 7812 www.stephenshouseandgardens.com

St Pancras Old Church, Pancras Road, London NW1
Tel: 020 7419 6679 www.posp.co.uk/old-st-pancras

Pollock's Toy Museum, 1 Scala Street, London W1
Tel: 020 7636 3452 pollockstoys.com

New London Architecture, The Building Centre, 26 Store
Street, London WC1
Tel: 020 7636 4044 www.newlondonarchitecture.org

Wesley's Chapel, 49 City Road, London EC1
Tel: 020 7253 2262 www.wesleyschapel.org.uk

Borough Market, 8 Southwark Street, London SE1
Tel: 020 7407 1002 www.boroughmarket.org.uk/

The View from the Shard, Railway Approach, London SE1
Tel: 0344 499 7222 www.theviewfromtheshard.com

Old Operating Theatre Museum, 9a St Thomas Street, London SE1
Tel: 020 7188 2679 www.thegarret.org.uk

Fashion and Textile Museum, 83 Bermondsey Street, London SE1
Tel: 020 7407 8664 www.ftmlondon.org

Bermondsey Antiques Market, Bermondsey Square, Greater London, SE13
bermondseysquare.net/bermondsey-antiques-market

Morden Hall Park, Morden Hall Road, Morden, London SM4
Tel: 020 8545 6850 www.nationaltrust.org.uk/morden-hall-park

Piccadilly Line

Charles Dickens Museum, 48 Doughty Street, London WC1
Tel: 020 7405 2127 www.dickensmuseum.com

Foundling Museum, 40 Brunswick Square, London WC1
Tel: 020 7841 3600 www.foundlingmuseum.org.uk

Horse Hospital, Colonnade, Bloomsbury, London WC1
Tel: 020 7833 3644 www.thehorsehospital.com

Brunei Gallery, SOAS, Thornhaugh Street, Russell Square, London WC1
Tel: 020 7898 4915 www.soas.ac.uk/gallery

London Film Museum, 45 Wellington Street, Covent Garden, London WC2
Tel: 020 7836 4913 www.londonfilmmuseum.com/home

London Transport Museum, Covent Garden Piazza,
London WC2
Tel: 020 7379 6344 www.ltmuseum.co.uk

Waterstones Piccadilly, 203-206 Piccadilly, London, W1
Tel: 020 7851 2400 www.waterstones.com/bookshops/piccadilly

St James Church, 197 Piccadilly, London, W1
Tel: 020 7734 4511 www.sjp.org.uk

Hatchards, 187 Piccadilly, London, W1
Tel: 020 7439 9921 www.hatchards.co.uk

Fortnum & Mason, 181 Piccadilly, London, WC1
Tel: 020 7734 8040 www.fortnumandmason.com

Burlington House, Piccadilly, London W1
Tel: 020 7300 8000 www.royalacademy.org.uk

Wellington Arch, Apsley Way, Hyde Park Corner, London W1
Tel: 020 7930 2726
www.english-heritage.org.uk/visit/places/wellington-arch

Apsley House, 149 Piccadilly, Hyde Park Corner, London W1
Tel: 020 7499 5676
www.english-heritage.org.uk/visit/places/apsley-house

The Vault, 150 Old Park Lane, London W1
Tel: 020 7514 1700
www.hardrock.com/cafes/london/memorabilia

Boston Manor House, Boston Manor Road, Brentford,
Middlesex TW8
Tel: 020 8568 2818 www.hounslow.info/arts-culture/historic-
houses-museums/boston-manor-house

Osterley Park, Jersey Road, Isleworth, Middlesex TW7
Tel: 020 8232 5050 www.nationaltrust.org.uk/osterley-park

Victoria Line

Walthamstow Market, 67 High Street, London E17
www.walthamforest.gov.uk/pages/servicechild/
walthamstow-market.aspx

Vestry House Museum, Vestry Road, London E17
Tel: 020 8496 4391 www.walthamforest.gov.uk/vestry-house

William Morris Gallery, Lloyd Park, Forest Road, Walthamstow,
London E17
Tel: 020 8496 4300 www.wmgallery.org.uk

Queen's Gallery, Buckingham Palace Road, London SW1
Tel: 020 7766 7300 www.royalcollection.org.uk/visit/the-
queens-gallery-buckingham-palace

Royal Mews, Buckingham Palace Road, London SW1
Tel: 020 7766 7334 www.royalcollection.org.uk/visit/royalmews

BBC Broadcasting House, Portland Place, London W1A
Tel: 0370 901 1227
www.bbc.co.uk/showsandtours/tours/bh_london

All Saints Church, 7 Margaret Street, London W1
Tel: 020 7636 1788 www.allsaintsmargaretstreet.org.uk

Westminster Cathedral, 42 Francis Street, London SW1
Tel: 020 7798 9055 www.westminstercathedral.org.uk

Tate Britain, Millbank, London SW1
Tel: 020 7887 8888 www.tate.org.uk/visit/tate-britain

Brixton Windmill, Windmill Gardens, Blenheim Gardens,
Brixton Hill, London SW2
www.brixtonwindmill.org

DLR

Ragged School Museum, 46-50 Copperfield Road, London E3
Tel: 020 8980 6405 www.raggedschoolmuseum.org.uk

Museum of London Docklands, No. 1 Warehouse,
West India Quay, London E14
Tel: 020 7001 9844 www.museumoflondon.org.uk/docklands

Billingsgate Fish Market, Trafalgar Way, Poplar, London E14
Tel: 020 7987 1118 www.cityoflondon.gov.uk/business/whole-
sale-food-markets/billingsgate/Pages/Tours-and-visits.aspx

Mudchute Farm, Pier Street, London E14
Tel: 020 7515 5901 www.mudchute.org

Cutty Sark, King William Walk, London SE10
Tel: 020 8858 4422 www.rmg.co.uk/cuttysark

The Fan Museum, 12 Crooms Hill, London SE10
Tel: 020 8305 1441 www.thefanmuseum.org.uk

Ranger's House and the Wernher Collection, Chesterfield
Walk, London SE10
Tel: 020 8294 2548 www.english-heritage.org.uk/visit/places/
rangers-house-the-wernher-collection/

Greenwich Heritage Centre, Artillery Square, London SE18
Tel: 020 8854 2452 www.greenwichheritage.org/site/index.php

Queen Elizabeth Olympic Park, 3 Thornton Street, London E2
Tel: 0333 800 8099
www.queenelizabetholympicpark.co.uk
www.Arcelormittalorbit.com

Overground

Harrow Museum, Headstone Recreation Ground, Pinner
View, Harrow HA2
Tel: 020 8863 6720 www.harrowmuseum.org.uk

Keats House, 10 Keats Grove, London NW3
Tel: 020 7332 3868
www.cityoflondon.gov.uk/things-to-do/attractions-around-
london/keats-house/visit/Pages/default.aspx

2 Willow Road, Hampstead, London NW3
Tel: 020 7435 6166 www.nationaltrust.org.uk/2-willow-road

Sutton House, 2-4 Homerton High Street, Hackney, London E9
Tel: 020 8986 2264 www.nationaltrust.org.uk/sutton-house

Geffrye Museum, 136 Kingsland Road, London E2
Tel: 020 7739 9893 www.geffrye-museum.org.uk

Horniman Museum, 100 London Rd, London SE23
Tel: 020 8699 1872 www.horniman.ac.uk

Dulwich Picture Gallery, Gallery Road, Southwark, London SE21
Tel: 020 8693 5254 www.dulwichpicturegallery.org.uk

Crystal Palace Park, Thicket Road, London SE19
Tel: 0300 303 8658
www.bromley.gov.uk/info/200073/parks_and_open_spaces/
780/about_crystal_palace_park

INDEX